# ETHICS IN MINISTRY

# ETHICS IN MINISTRY

## A Guide for the Professional

## WALTER E. WIEST
## ELWYN A. SMITH

Fortress Press/Minneapolis

ETHICS IN MINISTRY
A Guide for the Professional

Scripture quotations, unless otherwise noted, are from the Revised Standard Version of
the Bible, copyright © 1946, 1952, and 1971 by the Division of Christian Education of
the National Council of Churches.

Cover design: Ned Skubic

Library of Congress Cataloging-in-Publication Data

Wiest, Walter E., 1920–
    Ethics in ministry : a guide for the professional / Walter E.
Wiest and Elwyn A. Smith.
        p.   cm.
    ISBN 0-8006-2391-6
    1. Clergy—Professional ethics.   I. Smith, Elwyn A.   (Elwyn
Allen), 1919–   .   II. Title.
    BV4011.5.W54   1989
    241'.641—dc20                                                    89-35553
                                                                         CIP

The paper used in this publication meets the minimum requirements of American National
Standard for Information Sciences—Permanence of Paper for Printed Library Materials,
ANSI Z329.48-1984.                                                          ∞™

Manufactured in the U.S.A.                                              AF 1-2391

# Contents

129019

# Preface

This study intersperses discussion of ethical problems with case analysis. The content of the cases arises from the experience of the writers and those who have contributed less directly to this book: pastors with whom the authors have counseled, students, and colleagues. Most examples cited are composites; no single case describes an exact sequence of actual events. We have abbreviated and made modifications designed to serve the purpose of this book and to avoid disclosure. We avow our intention to hold in confidence all information disclosed to us confidentially.

Just as our subject matter has limits, so have we, the authors. We are white, Anglo-Saxon Protestant males. We acknowledge the limitations that these facts impose and we cannot presume to speak from the perspectives of American minorities, much less persons of the Third World. We reject all prejudice, whether racist and ethnic, sexist, or nationalistic. At the same time, we confess that such prejudices doubtless persist in our minds in conflict with our will in the matter. We believe that Christians from many quarters should share perspectives and listen seriously to each other. We hope that some of what we say here may be found useful to ministers in churches and ministries very different from those we know.

We write from a standpoint specifically Christian, without apology. At the same time, we know that we live in a world of many religious and nonreligious points of view that must understand and accept one another's right to live and teach. We believe that mutual acceptance and freedom are Christian principles. We address a very specific group of Christians, primarily the Protestant clergy, candidates preparing for this ministry, and others engaged in professional ministries who may not have clerical ordination (e.g., in Christian education, counseling, social work). We hope that our affirmations will not be taken for arrogance and indeed will interest some who do not share them.

Because the concerns of this book are so personal we think readers have a right to know some more specific information about ourselves. Theologically we are from Reformed backgrounds. At the same time, we are aware of how profoundly we are formed by the uniqueness of the twentieth century. We have been at one time and another pastor, professor, editor, and academic administrator. Neither of us has experienced divorce or widowhood and with our wives we have reared children—seven between us, four of them adopted. We are grandparents.

This book is written close to the end of our working careers and is an act of reflection, a profession of what we have come to believe, and an effort to fulfill our obligation to those who must live through times more difficult than ours. A review of the literature of ministerial ethics suggests that works like this are ephemeral. We only hope that the books that supersede this one will be better because of it.

*Walter E. Wiest*
*Elwyn A. Smith*

# Introduction

Little has been written recently to assist ministers of the Christian churches to resolve the complex professional problems that they face every day of the year.[1] This book deals primarily with *professional* ethics for clergy. The term "professional," as used here, has a broad application. In the Preface we mentioned that there are church professionals who may not be ordained as clerics. We mean to include them as equal partners in professional ministry. We have their interests in mind where we speak of "clergy" or "pastors." We hope that they will find what we say to be appropriate to them.

By professional ethics, we mean ethical issues arising in the ordinary practice of a profession, issues unique to or typical of that profession. David Luban's distinction in legal ethics is helpful here:

> When we think of lawyers' ethical lapses, we generally think of swindling and cheating, corner-cutting and client sell-outs. We think of ambulance-chasing and overbilling, chicanery and corruption. . . . Instead of such things, this volume is devoted to less conspicuous, more widespread and debatable practices such as a trial lawyer's effort to discredit an honest witness, fighting for a client's "right" to oppress or exploit, using technicalities to defeat justifiable claims.[2]

Professionals often do things that none will defend, such as sexual exploitation of a counsellee, client, or patient. Such gross violations of professional ethics usually conflict with fundamental ethical traditions that have developed for the defense of family, society, health, or human rights. They violate professional principle because they break with ethics at more fundamental levels. But there is a great deal more discussion of such ethical principles than there is of problems that arise only in the *practice* of the professions. While the kinship of professional ehics in the practice of ministry with fundamental ethics and with canons of ethical conduct that are shared by the professions is so close that the line cannot be drawn with the utmost strictness, we believe that abuse of a counsellee, client, or patient, whether sexual, psychological, financial, or of any other sort, is so intimately a part of the fundamental ethical questions of human relationships themselves that this book ought not duplicate the very competent literature available to any student. The vexing questions that arise in the daily life of a minister at work are sufficiently numerous and troubling to fill a book. It is to this kind of issue that this volume is specifically addressed.

We believe that Christian ministry has a social dimension that touches professional ethics very intimately at many points. Ministry takes place in a secular world and involves us in political and economic matters as well as churchly or religious ones. Most of these problems create obligations for Christians as such, including the clergy; but certain aspects of them pose questions to ministers that rarely confront laity in the churches. For example, given his or her workload in the congregation, how much time should a minister allocate to participation in a social protest that touches the welfare of thousands of the poor? In this book we deal not with the substantive social-ethical issue that creates such a problem but with the specific question of the ethics of time allocation. We do this not because time allocation is more important than the larger question of whether Christians shall act on behalf of the poor or sit on their hands—it is not—but because so little has been written to help the clergy think through this particular question in practice. At the same time there is a danger lest we get our heads down too far and too long and lose sight of the larger ethical context within which the professional questions must be answered. If that is allowed to happen, we lose our way on the professional question itself. There is constant dialogue between professional ethics, however specifically considered, and the more general ethical and social questions in which professional decisions are so often embedded and from which they frequently derive their significance.

This book is written from the standpoint of pastors and others with professional responsibilities in ministry whose congregations are part of a socially (but not legally) established order in the United States. Christian ethics requires that fundamental questions be raised about this and all other social orders, and we are keenly aware that there are many Christians abroad who see us as part of a system that oppresses them. Some of our own fellow citizens raise the same questions. These critiques should at a minimum galvanize thought about the justice of the way things are around us, much of which we would otherwise simply take for granted. A question hangs over us: should we be in this business of pastoral ministry at all, given the models that we accept?

The ethical quality of the social implications of our practice of the ministry is an encompassing condition of everything written here. It remains true, however, that the neglect of specifically professional issues in favor of more global ethical discussion does not serve our ministry well. We need to reflect on an admittedly more limited body of issues if we are to perform responsibly. This book may be seen as a part of the literature on the ethics of various professions—medicine, law, business—that has been developing in the past decade or two. As such, its subject matter is limited and specific.

There has been much discussion lately of problems of legal liability and insurance for clergy. There are significant ethical questions involved, but they cannot be discussed without exploration of legal problems that require the knowledge of experts in the law. Fortunately, some books are now available on the subject, and we refer readers to them.[3] Their coverage of the issues is much more adequate than could be provided here. We content ourselves with saying that while clergy would ordinarily be law-abiding and would surely want to avoid legal liability brought on either by ignorance or by irresponsible professional performance, they also are governed by ethical commitments that go beyond juridical law and that could on occasion call for incurring risk of legal penalty—such as a situation involving protection of confidentiality. Keeping out of trouble is a principle of prudence—but prudence is not the only, or perhaps even the right Christian principle to apply in every case.

### Approaches to Ethical Guidance

Ethical reflection is put to the test when positive values clash. A painfully common example is the occurrence of divorce in a minister's family. A pastor may be convinced that his/her marriage has become destructive to both partners and should in all honesty be ended. On the other hand, it may also be true that the congregation and perhaps the good repute of the church in the community will suffer if the minister is divorced. Resigning from the congregation may have very limited benefit. How should we approach such an ethical dilemma?

11

Readers may be inclined to expect a code of ethics, rules of professional conduct dealing specifically with the most common situations. Yet attitudes toward rules have changed considerably since 1960. At one time there existed among clergy a general sense that feasible rules of conduct could be formulated that were both good and useful. This sense reflected a respect for law that was deeply rooted in most Christian traditions, even those that have sharply attacked law when understood as a means of salvation. Today only too many consider the use of rules as inherently legalistic. Any reader of the Gospels must see that legalism—that is, the mentality that uses codes of law woodenly or casuistically—will not do. Rules can conflict, and if they are applied too rigidly and unexceptionally they can have unloving or unjust consequences.[4] But the protest against legalism should not be misconstrued as rejection of principles or rules as such. The Christian concepts of love and justice, for example, imply certain sorts of actions that are right most of the time. They hold good "as a rule."

The problem with prescribing codes as means of ethical guidance is that rules work best when they rest on consensus. They lose authority in a time when traditional norms are being questioned. In the kind of society that finds rules useful, most adults already know what can and cannot be tolerated. At the present time it is no longer true, for example, that "everybody knows that there cannot be divorced people in the ministry." A code of family ethics for clergy cannot resolve the present problem of clergy divorce because there has not yet emerged the necessary foundation in consensus.

From rule-making one can turn to more basic principles. One may state a principle in pure form, free of any specificity, or formulate it with reference to the conditions in which decisions are actually made. The principle for clergy in our example might be stated thus: "As faithful and obedient disciples of Christ, ministers must subordinate every personal consideration to the service of the gospel." Right! But it remains unclear just what a conscientious minister facing a domestic crisis is actually to do.

A principle may be stated with an eye to the problems of its application. "If in the judgment of the pastor (together with advisors and in relation to the church's doctrine and government) divorce would substantially handicap effectiveness, the pastor should seek another position or leave the ordained ministry." That way of putting this particular approach to ethical counsel has the virtue of bringing commitment to the ministry into the foreground and declares that the puzzlements of human behavior should be resolved in favor of vocation.

Professionals are people to whom work is crucial and they scarcely need to be reminded to grant it priority—although when emotion obscures judgment there is value in printing self-evident truth in clear black type. The principled guideline, as we might call this second approach, also has the merit of specificity. It flatly requires pastors to do an honest job of evaluating the effect of their personal decisions on congregational and community life, with their jobs on the block.

Joseph Fletcher's "situation ethics" advocates entire dependence on a single norm and rejects rules and guidelines altogether. "Just so you act in love. . . ." So high a principle creates an unbearable human burden. Who can be sure of knowing what love requires? Who can bring "love" objectively to bear upon an emotionally charged choice?

Then what sort of approach can be useful to the minister when troubling choices must be made?

## Responsible Thinking about Ethically Significant Decisions

Many specific ethical problems remain forever ambiguous. While this book contains many judgments on substance, we are principally concerned to communicate a way of thinking about conduct in relation to calling that we believe to be responsible even where honest differences must be respected.

Everyone comes to ethical choice furnished with basic points of reference. There is one's own conscience—what one can live with morally. There are also the vital interests of others: spouse, dependents, the congregation, professional colleagues, the profession itself. There is the practical need to behave in ways that make one employable.

There are also the materials of thought itself. In addition to the facts of the case, there is one's operative theology and the piety out of which one lives. Here we would place such points of reference as "the command of our Lord" or "the requirements of our calling." By calling a minister's theology and piety "the materials of thought" we do not suggest that these are purely subjective or personal. Far from it. Religious faith affirms that the ultimate realities, the immovables of our existence, even truth itself come to at least a partial expression in theology. Truth enters our lives in part as material of thought. Theology is not a matter of opinion. It is disciplined thinking about revelation and its implications for belief and action. It draws materials from other kinds of knowledge (philosophy, science, literature) but it always must ask, "Is this consistent with the essential content of Christian faith?"

There is also the emotional dimension of experience. Classical rationalists see emotion as a threat of distortion. We do not take that view. Every human being, whether illiterate or highly trained, operates out of an emotional structure that is a given. It grows and changes, it may undergo rupture, revolution, or renewal but it remains always true that no one decides anything, least of all the central questions of human existence, in the absence of emotion. We propose to take account of the psychological dimension of professional conduct without falling into an exclusively psycho-ethical approach.

Last among the perspectives in which we write is the social. This means first the church, that is, the universal Christian community in all its diversity, its denominational fellowships and traditions, and local congregational life. It also takes into account the social contexts in which each of these manifestations of the church exists and with which they interact in both desirable and undesirable ways.

## An Approach to Ethical Thinking

Ethical reflection is thinking about morality. We are intrinsically moral; we have consciences. Ordinarily we act upon moral principles that we take for granted. Sometimes we face situations that confuse us. We are not sure what is right. We are forced to think about our principles. Ethics is an effort to do such thinking systematically. Of course, ethical thought must also call upon feeling, sensitivity, and practical judgment about actions and their effects, so it is not possible to reduce the nuances of ethical thinking to a formula. How to think ethically is something that we will illustrate and analyze in the following chapters. Still, we want to suggest some preliminary steps to specifically ethical reflection that may be helpful:

1. *Be certain that there really is a problem.* Genuine problems require the application of appropriate disciplines—mathematics, psychology, and ethics, for example—but there are also mere appearances of problems. A problem may exist not so much in the environment of our work as in our feelings of discomfort in the presence of circumstances that alarm us. Just because we feel anxious does not mean there is a real problem "out there."

The first step of ethically responsible thought is to determine whether one's subjective responses are accurate. The signals of emotion are saying: "There is a problem here." Is there? Daniel Patrick Moynihan's celebrated medicine "Benign Neglect" might be the proper first dose! If one waits a bit and the signals die away, it may be that the "problem" was indicative of a digestive disorder rather than an objective ethical problem.

If we sometimes see a problem where there is none, we also sometimes see no problem where one exists. Instant solutions may be wrong, and can do damage. "There is no problem!" we may say. Or "It seems to me self-evident that. . . ." These often are not indicators of ethical thought but simply visceral reactions. Worse is the automatic "Christian reaction" like "I don't see how he can call himself a Christian and. . . ." Still worse is the assumption that one's own instant reaction is "Christian." To be compliant when a situation really calls for resistance, for instance, or to excuse rudeness by crowning it with the Christian virtue of candor are understandably human reactions. But they are no substitute for ethically serious thought.

2. *Get the facts.* How many times have we heard a sentence begin with: "Gosh, if I'd known. . . ." Facts do not exhaust truth and some relevant facts may elude the most persistent search, but a thorough scrutiny of data is essential to validate the thought and action that follow. If you're wrong on the facts, everything that follows is derailed.

3. *Determine the relevant theological principles.* We do not propose that you write a five-hundred-page theological prologomena about the conflict among the officers of the Board of Trustees! The fact is, however, that all responses betray our commitments and we ought to know what they are and be assured of their kinship with Christian belief. Your domineering church officer may have been getting more out of the church for years than he has given and his ego may badly need a trimming. Still, Christ has called the church to be his redeeming body, your troublesome elder has made a profession of faith that you have no solid ground to doubt, and God has not appointed the church to be a theater of clergy self-fulfillment any more than anyone else's. These are only a few of the theological principles of which a person who is committed to think ethically will be aware.

4. *Determine the relevant ethical principles.* Principles can become too abstract, but they should be the guidelines by which we decide how to act. Among other things, they help us to rise above conflicts between personalities by referring us to the ethical content of the gospel rather than to personal opinions, feelings, or likes and dislikes. Such conflicts arise between ministers and members of congregations. In fact, there is a principle for just such situations: the obligation to behave pastorally to a member whom one would in a grimmer mood happily feed to the alligators.

5. *Define your precise responsibilities in the matter at hand.* At one extreme is the tendency to feel that one is responsible for everything, with or without authority or power. At the other is a casuistic narrowing of responsibility to the point where the consequences of one's action are thrown on someone else. "What did he know and when did he know it?" was Senator Howard Baker's question during the Watergate hearings. That can be answered so narrowly that responsibility may be evaded even when a competent decision maker might have solved the problem handily with less than full knowledge. Thanks to moral formation, the clergy tend to take on more responsibility than they can feasibly discharge and this draws them toward authoritarian behavior, perpetual anxiety, and deteriorating personal relationships with their members.

6. *Be clear about the intention of the course of action you propose.* It is not only people who have intentions! Any program of action inevitably has a number of goals. If not reconciled and harmonized around a unifying intention, these can conflict and threaten the integrity of action. To be clear about intention has the further value of testing oneself for emotional bias. Your personal intention needs to harmonize with the thrust of the action.

7. *The church professional has an ethical responsibility to be effective.* To fly blind through a difficult problem on grounds that one's theological and ethical principles are correct is irresponsible. As genuinely resistant to solution as a problem may be, ineffectiveness is often in some degree an ethical shortcoming.

# PART ONE
# TRUTH

# 1

## What Is Telling the Truth?

In July of 1981 a Gallup poll was taken in which a cross section of Americans was asked how they rated persons of various occupations in regard to "honesty and ethical standards." Clergy were at the top of a list of about thirty occupational categories. Sixty-three percent of those surveyed ranked them high or very high, twenty-eight percent average, and only six percent low or very low (three percent had no opinion).

Pleasing as this may be, ministers may well have misgivings as to whether this high opinion is deserved. We know we face perplexities as to what is the honest and truthful thing to say or do in many situations.

Most of the questions pastors deal with have to do with telling the truth in the largest sense: the obligation to be honest in our communications, questions of how much of the truth to tell in differing circumstances, and the way in which the selecting and ordering of facts can distort truth in the telling. There is no way to grasp these issues apart from an understanding of basic ethical concepts and principles. These also provide groundwork for the analysis of other issues as well.

### Problems of Truth-telling

While ethical questions confront everyone and some questions faced by ministers are common to all professionals, certain problems are peculiar to the ministry. These range from a lack of honesty about what should be told, as with plagiarism in sermons, to what should not be told, as with the confidentiality issue.

Here is a range of typical pastoral dilemmas, all of which raise troubling questions about telling the truth.

*At a church-sponsored conference a minister preaches at the worship services that begin each day. Among those present is a prominent preacher whose sermons have appeared in print. One morning he is perplexed and then angry as he realizes that the sermon he is hearing is one of his own, delivered verbatim without acknowledgment. This is not the first time this has happened. He is concerned, not only for justice to himself but about the implications for the moral attitudes of the clergy. He has discovered that plagiarism is widespread. In a later discussion of ministerial ethics, he mentions this as a troubling and persistent problem.*

Plagiarism is a taking of credit for thoughts not one's own and is dishonest. It is dishonest not to tell a relevant truth: in this case, to credit the true author.

Lying by failing to tell the truth is not limited to plagiarism.

*The chairperson of a committee seeking to fill a position receives and reads a letter of recommendation from an applicant's pastor. The letter has nothing but good to report about the person. The chairperson tosses the letter aside impatiently, muttering: "These letters from clergy are all the same, all positive, all worthless. We never learn anything from them."*

Silence as lying may become a problem of conscience for a minister.

*Coming home from a meeting where there has been dispute about the church's stand on the doctrine of the divinity of Christ, a pastor reflects uneasily on the extent to which her views have changed since she was ordained. Also, in the course of some years of facing practical difficulties on the job, she has found that there are some tasks for which she doesn't seem to have a marked aptitude or even enthusiasm. She has begun to wonder about her fitness for the ministry. Does she still have a valid call? Is she perhaps just tired? Is all this change normal? Is she becoming a hypocrite? Has she an obligation to talk with someone about it?*

Prudence may require so much constraint of candor that ministers may wonder if dishonesty itself has not overtaken them.

*A pastor newly called to a congregation finds that the majority of his parishioners are much more conservative in their views than he on*

*some theological and social-ethical matters. He has warmed to the
people and wants to be their minister. In his own view, what he has
in common with them in Christian belief is a sufficient basis for
sound ministry. He knows, however, that many would be shocked
and offended if they knew some of his private thoughts and perhaps
his ministry would be rendered impossible. He feels that in time trust
and mutual affection can be built up which will enable him to deal
with these things more openly, but he cannot be sure of that.
Meanwhile, he feels dishonest. He tells himself that he would not lie
about his views if asked direct questions but when sticky issues arise
he finds himself temporizing, giving responses that he can tell himself
are honestly representative of his thinking but that may leave another
impression with his people. What is the honest thing to do?*

Silence as lying can complicate legitimate confidentiality, particularly
in counselling relationships.

*A teenage girl, relying explicitly on confidentiality, counsels with a
pastor concerning an affair she is having with an older man. The girl
does not want her parents to know and the pastor knows that these
parents would most likely react with horror, anger, and
condemnation. Nevertheless, they are responsible parents, loving
according to their own lights, and the daughter is involved in a
situation that could have devastating consequences. Her behavior is
also immoral in itself, shocking to both her family's and the church's
moral stance. Does confidentiality take precedence over the parents'
right to know?*

One cannot leap into questions where principles themselves collide
without establishing the theological and ethical perspectives from which
the issues are considered. Furthermore, ministers need a clear understanding of their own stance and so a sincerely held doctrine of the
ministry itself is required.

## The Minister and the Truth

Truth—which includes both truthfulness and being true—is the key
both to ministry and the ethics of ministry. Ministers of the gospel have
something to be true to. We have a message to proclaim that is given
to us, we do not make it up ourselves, and we are to witness to that
truth faithfully and with integrity. This is a moral commitment.

To be true to a profession requires a professional to acquire the
knowledge and skills necessary to uphold high standards of performance.

The scientist is committed to the honest pursuit of verifiable knowledge and the artist to works of genuine artistic quality. It is this moral element that makes sense of the definition of professionals as persons who profess something, who stand for certain values. As those who do professional ministry we are morally committed to an honest proclamation of the Christian faith, and to high standards of performance in the various tasks of ministry. We have a responsibility to do an honest job, which means acquiring the necessary knowledge and skills and being on our honor to use them well.

But there is more. The message we proclaim is itself the truth we receive in faith by the grace of God. It is the truth about God and about ourselves. It tells us that we are the image of God confused by the sin of rejecting God.

The truth tells us what we are to be and become. Yet it is more than something spoken or told; this truth is life itself, the new life offered us by God in Christ. This life goes beyond knowing to doing and being. It is embodied by him who said, "I am the Truth." This truth changes us and "trues up" our lives. In and by this truth we live in that mysterious exchange through which Christ abides in us and we in him. This truth makes us free, and very naturally expresses itself in our action. Truth is something we do as well as believe. To be ministers of this truth is to be animated by it, to proclaim what by grace we are. We do what we say. A contradiction between what we say and what we do is hypocrisy, to be sure. Worse, it is denial of the truth, Christ who is in us.

This living truth is also expressed as love, and love generates community. Ministry, or service (diakonia), belongs to community, to the church. The basis for all Christian ministry is the ministry of Christ, who came not to be served but to serve and to give his life for others. Service means more than waiting on others. It means caring about and for others.

While sin creates enmity and estrangement, the truth brings about reconciliation. It recreates community out of the Babel of our divided humanity. Through Christ we now have the "ministry of reconciliation" and have been appointed "ambassadors" with a "message" of reconciliation (2 Cor. 5:17-20). Instead of being, to use Luther's phrase, incurvatus in se, curved in upon ourselves, the truth takes us out of ourselves. Truth and love unite and transcend "Jew and Greek, barbarian and Scythian, slave and free, male and female" (Gal. 3:28).

The communal dimension of faith involves still another meaning of truth or truthfulness. Truth means being open to others. Community requires openness and honesty in relationships. There can be no genuine community between false selves. A community of hypocrites is a contradiction in terms. To be ministers is to be mediators of a truth that engenders and sustains true community.

In the light of these comments, we draw some conclusions. The first requirement of clerical ministry is that we be honest about our own faith. Obviously we cannot be ministers of this living truth if it is not part of us.

Second, clergy must forever be asking themselves if they are being true to the gospel in their preaching, teaching, and pastoral service. The questions we all face are familiar and constant. Am I motivated by my calling or by a desire for success? Do I preach the whole gospel or a lopsided one reflecting my own special preoccupations? Do I modernize too much? Alternatively, am I too traditional and resistant to change? Do I cater to the prejudices and preferences of my congregation, avoid or soft-pedal issues that might create controversy? If I do, is it really because I am concerned about the peace and unity of the church, or is that a rationalization of fear? When I do speak out, am I really being prophetic or merely arrogant and self-righteous? Is there more of me than of Christ in it all?

We are asking whether our ministry has integrity. That is, is it integrated around its proper center, the gospel? Does it hang together, have coherence, or is it loose-ended and inconsistent? Integrity also implies the commitment to standards of performance that are essential to a profession. To think theologically in a disciplined way both upon the essential content of faith and upon its implications for contemporary situations and problems requires theological competence. Also, to carry out our role in the life of the church, we need all the competence we can muster in the practical arts and techniques of pastoring. Slipshod work is a violation of ethical responsibility.

Finally, we need to reflect on specific ethical questions that are peculiar to the practice of clerical ministry. Every profession encounters questions peculiar to itself. The codes of professional ethics in law and medicine reflect a consciousness of the unique character of the problems in each field. They also reflect concern for integrity, the need to be true to certain values and standards.

## What to Do about the Truth

The starting point of the authors of this book was the bevy of questions typically encountered by practicing ministers. It is tempting to respond with detailed point-blank answers by producing a code. We have not taken that route. Some issues are so complicated that there is more than one conscientious judgment about what is right. It is necessary therefore to grasp the main stances of ethics itself. Without thorough grounding in theory there is no ethics. Christian morality is not just good gut reactions to situations; it is a process of thinking about what is right for Christians. In stating why we think truthfulness is basic to ministry, we have already begun to develop ethical guidelines that will be useful to our discussion of other issues as well. The rest of this chapter is devoted to a consideration of Christian ethical principles that apply to truth-telling. Application to practical situations comes in chapter 2. Through the balance of the book, theory and practice are more immediately interwoven.

Honest people, whether Christian or not, recognize honesty as a virtue and truth-telling as an obligation. They are necessary to the daily functioning of society. But different beliefs cause people to take significantly different positions. To determine the specifically Christian grounds for and understandings of honesty and truth-telling—that is, in order to deal with the examples we have cited—we need to understand how responsible thinkers and specifically Christian theologians have approached the questions of honesty and truth-telling.

There are two essays on truth-telling that have been used to show how differently Christians can think about such things. It will be helpful to consider them here to provoke our own thinking.

## Kant on the Truth

One answer to the problem of truthfulness is that we should *always* tell the truth, the whole truth, and nothing but the truth. Perhaps the best known presentation of this position is to be found in Immanuel Kant's classic essay, "On the Supposed Right to Lie from Altruistic Motives."[1] While Kant wrote as a philosopher, he was raised as a Christian, thought of himself as a Christian, and undoubtedly considered his ethics to be Christian.[2] Many Christians are swayed by his argument.

Kant defends this proposition: "It would be a crime to lie to a murderer who asked whether our friend who is pursued by him had taken refuge in our house."[3] Kant's answer is clear. One should tell the factual truth regardless of the consequences. This is in keeping with the whole character of Kant's ethical system. His view has often been called "duty for duty's sake." One's duty in various sorts of situations is defined by moral laws, which are to be obeyed unexceptionably. Kant was opposed to any ethics that first defined what is good and then justified any action useful to achieve these good goals (or to avoid those judged to be bad or evil). Such ethics, he felt, might justify wrong actions by appealing to the goodness of their results or consequences. For instance, one might justify stealing if one steals from the rich in order to give to the poor. One might justify an economic system in which a minority is kept in irremediable poverty if the overall effect is "the greatest good for the greatest number." One could justify the slaughter of large numbers of people if that might lead to a new and presumably better order of society, or defend lying if the lie protects someone from harm. Kant argues that an action can only be judged morally right if it is intrinsically right: i.e., if it contains in itself the right motivation (the "good will" is the only thing good in itself) and if it conforms to the rules or laws that define right actions. He rejects completely the notion that the end justifies the means.

This ethical point of view fits well with the Christian view that sees Christian morality as determined by the will of God and laid down in laws delivered from on high which are to be obeyed absolutely.[4]

Some Christians who do not fully accept Kant's position still may be disturbed because any exceptions to rules of Christian morality might result in undermining all moral restraints whatever. Once an exception is made, where can we stop? The fear is not only that logic seems to lead in this direction, although that is one cause for concern. Reasons offered for bending or breaking a rule in one case can readily be matched for another. Kant may be right: no exceptions.

Perhaps even more importantly, Kant protects against the fear that a critical psychological barrier will be breached. In society exceptions seem swiftly to destroy rules. One example of this is divorce. Within the memories of some of us, divorce was basically out of the question in most parts of our society. Divorced persons lived under a cloud and in many families no divorce had ever occurred. But obstacles to divorce began to fall in the period just after World War I and, one might argue, now look where we are! Our purpose here is not to debate the causes of a rising divorce rate but to acknowledge that many people are convinced that things fall apart once exceptions begin to multiply. Their concern should not be taken lightly, and we shall take it seriously.

We suppose that most pastors would agree, however, that Kant's rigid rule will not serve in many situations. Most of us would withhold the truth or even tell a lie to save the life of a friend. More to the point in pastoral experience, we face conflicts of conscience frequently. What of cases in which we owe it to one person to keep something in confidence while there are others who would be affected by what we know and seem therefore to have a right to know?

Neither would we agree that just anyone has the right to know on demand, as Kant seems to think. Further, any pastor knows numerous situations in which telling the whole truth would hurt and alienate and do little or no good. Our problem here is to decide when we are skirting the truth not because it would be truly inappropriate to tell it but simply because it would be painful. When we waffle, Kant is there to remind us of our *prima facie* obligation to tell the truth. But then, he was not looking at the problem through a pastor's glasses!

> *Pastor A. has been asked to write a reference for a friend and member who is applying for a teaching position. The applicant could be recommended on all counts except one. A single man, the candidate has sexual affairs from time to time. He is discreet; only a handful of friends know and they do not talk about it. The minister knows because he is both friend and pastor. The two have discussed the moral issue of this behavior frankly but without agreement. The candidate has always kept his sexual practices isolated from his work and has never tried to influence his students in favor of this aspect of his life-style. His moral influence on students has been good, better than most. These affairs seem inconsistent with his friend's general standard of behavior and Pastor A. regards him as a sound person.*
>
> *The minister also suspects that the principal and school board would probably not hire his friend if they knew about his sexual behavior. The minister's judgment is that the school could do a great deal worse, all things considered. Yet if his letter of recommendation says that the applicant is of good moral character, coming from a clergyperson this will be understood by the school people to mean that the pastor knows of no such behavior.*

What is the honest thing to do?

St. Paul has advice for us. On the one hand, he said we should "speak the truth in love" (Eph. 4:15). On the other, he indicated that we should do and say what "edifies" or "builds up" community and the persons in it (1 Cor. 14:4, 26). Concerns of this sort commit us to honesty in relationships and a community of love and grace should be able to tolerate more honesty than most. Yet speaking "the truth, the whole truth, and nothing but the truth" can sometimes be unloving and destructive. Indeed, it may even express more of sinful egoism than of the love of Christ.

The problems about truth-telling that this raises are more helpfully addressed by Dietrich Bonhoeffer, especially in his essay "What Is Meant by Telling the Truth?"[5]

## Bonhoeffer on the Truth

Bonhoeffer was a devout Christian and a biblically oriented theologian whose views on this subject are substantially opposite to those of Kant. For him truth is not only the actual facts of a case but above all "the living truth between human beings." In any situation it is the quality or character of the relationship between persons and what actually happens in their responses to each other that matter ethically. This "living reality" varies with the different sorts of situations and relationships in which people find themselves. It is not surprising, then, to find Bonhoeffer saying that "telling the truth" can be different according to the particular situations in which one stands at different times. Account must be taken of one's relationships at each particular time. This also means that one must determine who is entitled to what truth, or what part of it, in each case. (This principle Kant explicitly rejects.) For instance, some things that one is obligated to share within one's family are not to be shared with others. Bonhoeffer uses the illustration of a child who is asked by the teacher in front of the class whether it is true that his father often comes home drunk. The child denies it, although it is true. Bonhoeffer maintains that the child has done nothing morally wrong, since the question had to do with a family matter and the teacher had no right to ask it.

Here we encounter one of the two basic concepts that affect the interpretation of truth-telling in Bonhoeffer's essay. The first is that of the "orders of life" or "mandates," as Bonhoeffer calls them elsewhere in his book *Ethics*. Human "living reality" is a reality that God creates and it is structured so that certain functions, certain kinds of authority and responsibility, are assigned to the state, the economic order (work), the family, the church. The individual has different moral obligations to the various orders. The state, for instance, has no right to interfere with what properly belongs to family or church (a point of obvious significance to Bonhoeffer, who was struggling against the totalitarian Nazi regime). Like the school child, we have no obligation to tell some truths to those who have no right to demand them.

Truth-telling is also affected by the relative positions persons have within the orders of life. As Bonhoeffer saw them, these relationships are ordered very hierarchically. A child, for example, should have its life "open before the parents" whereas parents are not to expose so much of their lives to the child. Bonhoeffer believed in a more hierarchical ordering than many Americans find desirable. Surely it is correct, however, that our ethical responsibilities are affected by the roles we play within community and institutional structures. In school life, for example, ethical responsibility differs among teacher, student, and administrator. So with wife, husband, and child in the family, or pastor and parishioner in church life.

The second concept that affects Bonhoeffer's analysis is the reality of sin. Sin causes the representatives of one order to encroach on the territory of others. Sin creates disunity and conflict. In Christ, God has introduced the new reality of redemptive and reconciling love that works toward unity and harmony.[6] But sin obviously is still with us and we must live and act within "both the inner contradiction and the inner consistency of the real." It is the recognition of this dimension of contradiction that causes Bonhoeffer to assert that it can be a moral duty to practice deception: for instance, toward an enemy in time of war. He consequently rejects the definition of a lie as "the deliberate deception of another to [that person's] detriment." To call such acts "lies" would be to claim that they are always morally wrong by definition.

Bonhoeffer does not take this position lightly. We may discern between the lines the inner anguish he felt about the constant deception that he had to practice during his involvement in resistance to the Nazis during World War II, as reflected in his *Letters and Papers from Prison*. He was anguished not only over his implication in the violence of war and the plot to assassinate Hitler but also over having to "live a lie" from day to day. The profound pain of this can be understood if we remember that truth for Bonhoeffer is a "living truth between human beings" characterized by love, trust, and honesty. One cannot enter into a genuine relationship with others when one is constantly dissimulating. When one's own integrity is threatened and strained, furthermore, one's very selfhood is undermined. And yet, in a sinful world, situations occur in which such things cannot be avoided by active and morally responsible people.

Bonhoeffer makes one more point about the effects that the sinful conditions of life have upon truth-telling. Some of our faults and weaknesses should be allowed to remain covered by the decent cloak of silence. It is the cynic, he says, who delights in hurting or destroying people by claiming that his unwavering devotion to speaking the truth forces him to expose all human weaknesses. Such a person "is destroying the living truth between [persons]. He wounds, shames, desecrates mystery, breaks confidence, betrays the community in which he lives, and laughs arrogantly at the devastation he has wrought and at the human weakness that 'cannot bear the truth.' " By the same token, we should not be too quick to confess all our own faults publicly. A decent reticence is necessary to dignity and to healthy relations with others.[7]

## Balancing Ethical Principles

Before we seize upon Bonhoeffer's interpretation of truth-telling in order to escape some of the dilemmas of ministerial ethics, we must see the danger that lies in stressing truth as the "living reality between persons" at the expense of factual truth, of "veracity." Paul Lehmann, in elaborating on Bonhoeffer's essay, seems to us in such danger. He poses a situation that helpfully illustrates the relativity of truth-telling in many cases. Suppose one has a car one wants to sell. Is one morally obligated to tell the whole factual truth about the car (as far as one knows it) to each and every prospective buyer? Lehmann proposes that moral obligation would vary with the circumstances. "Telling the truth about the car would obviously not be identical with *optimum verbal veracity.* It would be different for a high school adolescent and for a man in middle life; for a man who had two cars and for a man who had to dispose of the only car he had in order to pay for his wife's burial; for a humanist and for a Christian."[8]

Lehmann agrees with Bonhoeffer that the relationships in which we stand to others, determined within and between the "orders" of our common life, must be taken into account in deciding what truth is to be told in any given case. But he goes further than Bonhoeffer appears to intend. In any situation, says Lehmann, including a business trans- action, telling the truth consists of speaking the right word or the living word which is "instrumental" to the "openness of human beings to each other." "If the buyer and seller of this car come through the transaction to a true consideration of each other's predicament, and so are linked to each other as human beings, then they do not merely transact business. The business transaction becomes instrumental to their dis- covery of each other as human beings, and whether much or little is told about the car, whatever is told is the truth. It is this *human* factor . . . which is the definitely *ethical* factor."[9]

Before criticizing Lehmann, we should note the extent to which we actually behave as he suggests in his illustration. Suppose one is about to sell one's car to a close friend. It would be very odd if one were not much more scrupulous in telling the whole truth about the car in such a case. Most of us would be less scrupulous with a total stranger and still less with a car dealer on a trade-in. There would be different factors involved in each case: they are different sorts of relationships. With the friend, friendship itself would be at stake. The car dealer will have a mechanic check out the car. With a stranger, friendship would not be involved, although if the buyer were a widow with three children to support and who needed the car to hold her job, one's reaction would be different than if the sale were being made to a wealthy father who buys a car for each of his children as they reach driving age.

Lehmann's theories are practiced every day. But he distorts the truth by saying it is entirely a matter of the "living relationship" that underlies the transaction and "whatever is told is the truth" as long as a genuine interpersonal relationship somehow happens. Veracity, in some appropriate form, is necessary to honesty and trust in a good relationship. It is hard to see how a relationship could survive the later disclosure of a deliberately concealed but major fault in a car sold by a charming salesperson. Veracity is in some sense morally right in itself; we should always feel a constraint toward it, even if we find it inadvisable to tell all we know. Kant, commenting upon that constraint, said, "If one is asked whether he intends to speak truthfully in a statement that he is about to make and does not receive the question with indignation . . . but rather asks permission to consider possible exceptions, that person is already potentially a liar."[10]

Kant is right to this extent: there must be a moral presumption of veracity. As a rule we are expected to tell the factual truth pertinent in a given case. If there are exceptions, Kant persuades us to be careful about them. Exceptions must remain truly exceptional. The justification given for false or misleading statements in an extraordinary situation also cannot be used to justify misrepresentation generally. (Bonhoeffer is very insistent about this.) We should feel constrained to tell the factual truth, be uneasy about not telling it, and recognize that all exceptions require special justification unique to each situation.

This demonstrates the need to have the principle of veracity built into us as a virtue: a deeply rooted inner predisposition to tell the factual truth. It is so easy to rationalize, to invent excuses and justifications that are convincing especially as long as we keep them to ourselves. How would they look if we had to explain them to the world?[11] If we are to be honest with others we must be honest with ourselves and being dishonest with others ends in falsifying ourselves. This is the point from which we enter the issues of integrity and hypocrisy.

Bonhoeffer's intention was not to undermine literal or factual truth; instead, he maintained that veracity is one consideration in a larger living situation and that this living reality includes variable personal and social relationships and circumstances. Moral responsibility is affected by them, he believed, and moral truthfulness is being true to the requirements of responsible relationships. What we say, including the elements of factual truth we are to tell, must be governed by this requirement to be true to the person and the facts.

Bonhoeffer's struggle with a sense of guilt over the deceptions necessary in the resistance movement shows that he did not discount their ethical significance.[12] In fact, he has a good deal to say elsewhere about the necessity of accepting a degree or kind of guilt as part of the price of doing the right thing in such extreme situations.[13] His own judgment about what he did could be summarized in the phrase "right, but guilty." Yet he disagreed fundamentally with Kant. In Bonhoeffer's view, deception is required in exceptional cases. The truth (or a part of it) that one is required to tell varies with circumstances and persons who have differing claims upon the truth we tell. Kant allows neither of these distinctions.

The exceptional case is often one in which two principles ordinarily in harmony with each other are irreconcilable. For example, one principle of loving Christian responsibility calls for veracity. But another calls for avoiding what would do physical harm to others. When it comes to telling a would-be murderer where his victim is hiding, the two principles conflict. One must take priority. But a third principle gives us necessary guidance, that is, special obligations to a friend. Therefore, in making an exception we are not acting capriciously or arbitrarily, nor substituting "expediency" (Kant's word) for moral obligation. Neither are we rescinding the rule of veracity; it will still hold good "as a rule." Rather, we are following another rule or guideline, also an intrinsic part of our morality, which takes priority in this case. This should be reassuring to those who worry about uncontrollable consequences of breaking rules.

Many of the problematic situations of ministerial ethics can be analyzed in this way. Such decisions cannot be made rigidly by consulting a rule book. Helped by grace and the Holy Spirit, we must take into consideration the good of the people involved in particular situations. There is no avoiding risk in such cases. This risk we must assume in responsible freedom, for there is no purely objective method of determining which rule should take priority or what is unquestionably the right thing to do. Bonhoeffer has some challenging comments to make on the need for Christians to accept, not to dodge, their free responsibility in Christ at such moments.[14]

## The Biblical Base

The contrasting positions of Kant and Bonhoeffer show a spectrum of the principles and guidelines that may be used to address issues of truth-telling, the subject of the next chapter. Before proceeding to discussion of cases, however, we must ask whether these guidelines are consistent with Scripture. What does the Bible have to say, explicitly or implicitly, about truth-telling?

Biblical ethics includes a principle of veracity which is more prominent in the New Testament than in the Old Testament. In both Testaments, however, veracity is placed within the context of a larger concept of truth. It is to this larger concept that we must appeal when rules collide or when it is not immediately obvious how they should be applied.

In the Old Testament, the basic word for truth is 'emeth (âman, 'emunah in other forms). It means something firm, unchanging, lasting, and therefore reliable, trustworthy, faithful. It is above all a characteristic of God who is "the God of truth." The term is often coupled with hesed—steadfast love. This indicates not only that God can be depended upon to be unfailingly loving but also that truthfulness is to be contrasted with fickleness more fundamentally than with lying or deception. All the same, God would not lie.

In Scripture the concepts of covenant and truth are closely interconnected. Truthfulness is intrinsic to God's covenants with people, in which God makes trustworthy promises and is unvaryingly faithful to covenantal stipulations. In response to God's faithfulness the covenant people are also to be faithful in their inner commitments, as well as in their external actions. They are, of course, to obey God's will, as indicated in laws and commandments. More than that, they are to "speak the truth from [the] heart" (Ps. 15:2) and have the law "written on the heart" (as in Jeremiah and Ezekiel). As the outward expression of this they are to "walk in the truth" or "in faithfulness," in 'emeth (2 Kings 20:3, also 1 Kings 2:4; Ps. 26:3), and have "truth in the inward being" (Ps. 51:6). The relationship is one in which one's whole being is caught up; it is "ontological," as Otto Piper says. Faithfulness is not just "cognitive," having to do with knowledge or with veracity. 'Emeth "designates the whole field of religious and moral life." Its opposite is not just lying but any unrighteousness or unfaithfulness to God.[15]

In the New Testament, veracity plays a much larger role. Truth (*alētheia*) regularly means what is factual or real, and to speak falsely is to misrepresent the facts. But there is also a larger meaning that builds upon the Old Testament *'emeth*. The relationship between God and people in the covenant is now translated into the new relationship brought about in Jesus Christ. In many New Testament passages *alētheia* means "the content of Christianity as the absolute truth"[16] or "the Christian revelation, the truth as revealed by Christ."[17]

Revelation of truth means also salvation, the transformed life in Christ. This is the "word of truth" or the "truth of the gospel." It is the Word of God that is embodied in Christ. It is, therefore, also the truth of Christ, and can be identified with Christ (e.g., John 14:6).[18] We in turn are to have faith in the truth (*pisteuein*, be wholly committed to it). This is the truth in which we are to walk (*peripatein*), and which we are to *do* (John 3:21, 1 John 1:6). It is the truth that makes us free (John 8:32); free from sin, fulfilled in our humanity. In it, we "know God and live a good life."[19]

As in the Old Testament, truth in the New Testament is contrasted not just with lying or hypocrisy but with any sinful or disobedient action. Being truthful means "complying with the will of God." Complying is not primarily a matter of our accepting certain propositions about God and righteousness and then drawing logical conclusions about what we are to do (although this is part of our response and not to be scorned in itself). Rather, there is a "divine impulse" that moves us and that is "actualized" by our faith response. The truth then is "in us"; we are "of the truth"; it "becomes our very nature." Truth becomes imperative; we are to "do the truth." In so doing, we are energized by the grace and Spirit of God.[20]

Doing the truth, complying with the will of God, also means having the right attitudes and dispositions toward our fellow human beings. God's truth provides impetus for loving and reconciled relationships. Lying is destructive of such relationships, as is hypocrisy. But for Christians ethical responsibility is above all a matter of a loving relationship to God and loving concern for our neighbor. We are brought into a community of faith and reconciliation, the church. We are also to love all neighbors and, indeed, even our enemies. Veracity is enjoined "as a rule," but there are times when appeal must be made beyond the law to what love requires in a particular case.

One of the most familiar examples in the New Testament of the appeal to love beyond the law—one that often applies to ministerial ethics—is the Gospel account of Jesus' setting aside of the Sabbath laws on certain occasions. There are a number of such episodes recorded in all four Gospels. Various reasons are given for Jesus' actions. Perhaps the most familiar is in Mark 2:27: "The sabbath was made for [human beings], not [human beings] for the sabbath." This can be understood to mean that the Sabbath laws had an overarching and justifying purpose: they were intended for the well-being of humankind. If they had been rigidly obeyed in the case of the disciples' picking corn to allay hunger, their very purpose would have been negated.

We could add to this all of the excoriations of rigid legalism that pervade both the Gospels and the Pauline writings. From St. Paul, however, we should add one more ethical guideline derived from 1 Corinthians 10, in which St. Paul draws his conclusions about a controversy between Jewish and gentile Christians. The issue was whether it was permissible to eat the flesh of animals used in non-Christian religious sacrifices before being sold in the market. In dealing with the problem, St. Paul first asserts that nothing in God's creation is intrinsically evil; therefore, nothing is forbidden. St. Paul uses these statements to back up his argument: "The earth is the Lord's and everything in it" (1 Cor. 10:26) and "All things are lawful (1 Cor. 10:23)." What is more, we have the freedom in Christ to exercise our own consciences in such matters. St. Paul concludes: "Why should my liberty be determined by another [person's] scruples?" (1 Cor. 10:29).

We are constrained by another consideration: "Let no one seek his own good, but the good of his neighbor" (1 Cor. 2:4). We must have regard for what is constructive in its effects on others and on the life of the community. Although St. Paul gives not an inch in regard to his right to his own conscience, he not only tolerates the differing scruples of others but declares that if they are made known to him in any situation he will defer to them: that is, he will not eat the meat. The guideline we draw from this is that there are some issues in which Christians must allow for honest differences of judgment as to what is right, and must honor and protect each others' right to differ. In this way, liberty is constrained, not by legalistic "do's" and "don'ts," but by the regard for other people that takes priority in Christian morality.

Even when informed by Christian faith and illuminated by Scripture, there will always be issues and decisions that remain ambiguous. Limits and guidelines will help us to determine an acceptable range of defensible actions. Options beyond that range can be excluded. We must be prepared to acknowledge alternative views within that range that are held by other Christians, and must defend these Christians' right to hold them even though we ourselves find another view to be right. This observation will apply to some of the cases involving the ethics of truth-telling in ministry, to which we shall now turn our attention.

# 2

## How We Tell the Truth

In the following chapter, we will examine five issues involving truth-telling that may cause ethical dilemmas for church professionals in some phase of their ministry. In each of these areas, the ethical principles that help guide our decisions and actions will be discussed.

### Plagiarism

The case of plagiarism presented at the beginning of the last chapter is an actual one. Unfortunately, it is only one of many. Codes of ministerial ethics usually include this issue. Many will remember a well-publicized court case in which it was revealed that a prominent preacher, recently deceased, had plagiarized a number of his sermons from another preacher's published works. A suit was brought against the estate.

Perhaps the first thing to be said about plagiarism is that because of copyright laws it is illegal to use published writings. Legalities aside, the practice is dishonest and morally wrong. We shall examine what precisely is wrong with it and why it happens.

The most common causes of plagiarism are not sheer laziness or deliberate dishonesty, even though ministers are not exempt from such motives. A common situation that tempts us to misappropriate others' work is that of pastors who, under pressure all week from other tasks, come up on Saturday without a sermon or even a usable idea for one. So they reach desperately for available material.

Most ministers are busy rather than lazy or idle. People expect much of them and they demand much of themselves. A contributing cause of plagiarism is our failure to distribute limited time and energy properly among demands worthy and more or less pressing. Ministers who do not reserve time for reading and theological study find that the well runs dry. To be sure, study alone does not produce effective sermons. Good preaching arises from interaction between the practical experience of ministry and theological reflection. One evidence of the importance of study, however, is the reaction of pastors who have entered Doctor of Ministry programs and thus are doing substantial reading for the first time in a long while. Many testify that as an immediate and visible effect of renewed study, their parishioners are responding to their sermons more appreciatively. One pastor remarked: "My wife tells me that in the past two months she has been really listening to my sermons for the first time in twenty years!"

When the well is dry, however, the voice of temptation is heard: "Is it really so wrong to borrow? The important thing is that my people be fed, and this will do it. Does it really matter what the source may be?" The choice of rationalizations is infinite. In some cases, all rationalization may be smothered by panic and it may simply come down to "grab and run." Some ministers succeed in rationalizing the act itself at so profound a psychic level that they convince themselves they have not really copied another's words at all. This phenomenon has been observed in seminary students. At least one puzzled professor, upon confronting certain students with their offenses, was amazed to find them reacting with innocent surprise and maintaining stoutly that they had been unaware of what they had been doing. Initially, the professor put this down as a transparent attempt to brazen it out. In time, he became convinced that the students, under pressure of time and suffering from a lack of confidence in their ability to handle the assignment, had slipped by stages from depending heavily upon sources into actually copying them, masking from themselves what they were doing and ultimately repressing awareness altogether. Their protestations of innocence were unfeigned, although wholly groundless.

Whatever role pressures and anxieties play, ministers and theological students frequently do not really understand the proper use of literary sources and how to distinguish right from wrong in their use.

We can offer some guidance by beginning with a definition of plagiarism. To plagiarize is "to steal and use (the ideas or writings of another) as one's own."[1] Plagiarism has to do with the improper appropriation of both another's words and another's ideas. The problem of use of words is not quite as complicated as the use of ideas. Whenever one uses phrases or sentences verbatim from another's writing, the source should be named and credit given, the oral equivalent of quotation marks and footnotes.

The use of individual words presents more of a problem. Some words are basic to a Christian theological vocabulary and do not have to be credited to anyone in particular even though one may have been prompted to use them by recent reading. Others may have been given special meaning in a particular published work, in which case credit should be given if one wishes to make use of the special insight of the writer. For instance, one of the present authors has used H. Richard Niebuhr's special interpretations of the common terms "monotheism," "henotheism," and "polytheism" in a sermon.[2] Although his own further interpretations and applications were made, credit was given.

A more difficult problem is that plagiarism is also defined as using others' ideas as though they were one's own. Here there are shadowy, uncertain areas. A few guidelines may be suggested. Insights drawn from commentaries for the interpretation of a text or biblical passage may be used fairly. Unless verbatim quotations are included, credit need not be given. Theological ideas or insights that are widely disseminated need not be credited to a particular thinker. For instance, Reinhold Niebuhr made much of his interpretation of sin as self-centeredness or self-interest. So have many others, with various twists of interpretation. In using such ideas one should give specific credit only when using an interpretation unique to a theological writer.[3] Reading others' sermons can be helpful as a stimulus to homiletical imagination and a help to style. It also provides the material of temptation.

The real answer to the subtle pressures to plagiarize is to give adequate time to reading that can become the material of one's own thought. The broadening and deepening of a preacher's own theological and homiletical resources result from thoughtful reading, not from borrowing. If direct appropriation is kept to a minimum, the rule should be: "When in doubt, give credit."

Worst of all is the plagiarizing of a whole sermon either verbatim or with minor changes in wording. Also wrong is the wholesale borrowing of the main ideas or points of a sermon without acknowledgment, even with changes in wording, when those changes do not materially affect the substance of the sermon.

Plagiarism is a greater concern in modern Western culture than it has been in other times and places. As with truthfulness in general, there are differences between current cultural standards and specifically Christian ones. We can conjecture about the sources of modern sensitivities to plagiarism. Wide dissemination of printed materials combined with popular education have created a large enough readership so that writers can make a living by their publications. The capitalist notion of private property has been extended to include ideas, resulting in patent and copyright laws; consequently, imitating published ideas is equivalent to stealing tangible property. This means not only stealing part of another's means of livelihood but also something of that person's honor and prestige. Scientific method has no doubt also contributed to modern understandings of plagiarism. Experimental results and new theories are published so they can be verified by other scientists. Linked to this is the belief that the individual discoverer should be given credit. Not only Nobel prizes but also promotion and tenure depend on such credit.

Christianity is not necessarily tied to or bound by such cultural relativities. For instance, we regularly give credit to St. Paul when we make use of his interpretations of Christian belief. But it is difficult to imagine St. Paul himself being concerned about getting such credit in anything like the way modern Western scholars are. If anything, St. Paul was interested in getting people to appropriate his ideas as freely and fully as possible!

The first ethical concept that applies to plagiarism is basic to veracity itself: the "living reality" between persons. This has a special application to the relation between pastor and people. Theologically understood, preaching is a happening in which God is graciously present and redemptively active. Over this aspect of preaching we have no control. We rely on divine promises. In the human dimension, preaching brings to special expression and intensification the living relationship between pastor and people. It is essential to this transaction that the participants be authentically present to each other, not hiding behind false faces or artificial roles and poses or hypocritical professions of faith. If the sermon is represented as having been written by the pastor when it has not been, falseness intrudes.

The English Puritans made this point when they objected to a practice required in the Church of England by Queen Elizabeth I.[4] She had decreed that preaching should be done only by reading homilies prepared by the hierarchy and distributed to the local clergy. The Puritans did not object to the theological content of the homilies, which was generally acceptable to them. Rather, it was based on their concept of preaching. The prepared homilies "lacked life," they claimed. The practice did not allow ministers to preach to the particular needs, faults, and responsibilities of the members of local congregations.

Preaching is meant to be part of a continuing vital dialogue between pastor and people who are together a people of God in Christ, engaged with each other at the deepest and most authentic level of their beings. A preacher who violates this covenant by plagiarizing is falsifying the relationship of pastor and people and failing to meet the needs of the people. True, a particular plagiarized sermon may speak to the needs of the people on a single occasion. But getting away with it occasionally does not justify the act morally, any more than getting away with an illegal action makes the action really legal. And plagiarism is devastating when it is habitual.

The principle of veracity itself is directly betrayed by plagiarism. Truth-telling involves both the truthfulness of what is said and the honesty of the person saying it. These might be called the objective and subjective poles of truth-telling. The objective pole is the content of what is spoken and the subjective pole is the speaker. Dishonesty occurs either when the content is false or when speakers misrepresent themselves by taking credit for words or ideas not their own. Veracity is always present in genuine selfhood and is essential to the "living reality" of loving relationships.

When we speak of the specifically Christian grounds for refusing plagiarism we do not mean to imply that all the considerations we mention are unique to Christian ethics. Some non-Christian or non-religious ethics make similar affirmations although their foundational reasons are different. Christians who live in Western culture must also take into account their social situation and the going moral and legal standards. Where livelihood and professional status depend on published writing, for example, misappropriation of words and ideas is a form of theft. Civil laws often express and incorporate minimal moral standards. [5] While there are conditions under which Christians may be called upon to disobey laws for ethical reasons, laws that defend against plagiarism clearly do not call for such disobedience. The intention of laws that protect only printed materials should be respected by clergy in regard also to unpublished sermons.

## Letters of Recommendation

We have warned that there are many issues of ethics in regard to which there is genuine uncertainty and room for honest differences of judgment. Writing recommendations is one such issue. While a range of views may be defined within which legitimate choices are allowable, outside this, most views and actions must be ruled out. No one is helped by the recommender who has nothing but good to say. Those to whom references are addressed are not impressed by letters that are clearly uncritical. At the other extreme, we remember Bonhoeffer's warning against the destructiveness of pointing out every fault under cover of being honest. It is expected that in a letter of recommendation one will say as much as possible that is positive and as few negative things as honesty allows. What is crucial is that the truth should be told where it really counts, as kindly as possible. Thus the failure to mention a negative factor that is crucial in the job consideration falls outside the range of the ethical.

Pastors and church professionals are sometimes asked for references for persons about whose professional competence they can make no accurate judgment. What prospective employers and other addressees expect of the ministers is an evaluation of the subject's moral character and personal traits, with church membership and participation probably considered as adjunct to morality. In writing recommendations for fellow ministers or students applying to professional schools, comments on professional competencies or aptitudes will also be in order.

We are bound to be honest with the party to whom the recommendation is addressed. We accept this obligation implicitly when we agree to write the letter. At the same time, we have obligations to the person about whom we are writing. This sometimes presents clear conflicts of responsibility; more often there are obscure areas in which it is difficult to judge whether there is a conflict or not. Furthermore, the recipient of the recommendation has responsibilities and one cannot be sure how well these will be met. If a letter is written in confidence, will confidentiality be preserved? If the recipient is a committee, will the information be disseminated? If the recommendation goes to someone in an organization where such things are filed and may be computerized, who will have access to the information down the road? Persons about whom information is supplied often have the right to demand access to their files. What then?

Bonhoeffer reminds us that the truth to be told varies with circumstances and that one must distinguish among parties as to their claims on the truth. Some things we know about persons are clearly protected by pastoral or counseling confidentiality. Some are not so clearly protected, and may be relevant to the request for a letter of reference.

In chapter 1 we posed a situation in which a pastor was asked to recommend a teacher whom he knew to have had occasional sexual affairs. Should the pastor reveal this fact to the hiring committee? This is an example of a sure "loser"; the committee will fully expect the pastor to tell it about any such trait while the person recommended will expect the pastor to keep such information confidential. One or another is sure to feel that the pastor has been less than honest or fair.

When the person being recommended is also a parishioner, the question also touches pastoral care. Along with the risk that a member's trust may be destroyed, there are also important pastoral opportunities. Perhaps this presents an occasion for a searching discussion of morals. Yet this is not possible unless a minister has already fostered strong pastoral bonds. There is a case for letting the appointing committee make the judgment as to the relevance of this man's sexual conduct. The pastor who comes to this choice with pastoral groundwork well laid can put the issue before his member and create the occasion for a more profound discussion of ethics, personal and professional, than would otherwise have been possible. The possibility of responding at the highest ethical level is often denied the pastor who has not been thorough in developing strong pastoral relationships with the people.

What are the components, the principles and guidelines, that figure in responsible ethical thinking in cases such as this?

In any situation, veracity—simply telling the truth honestly and candidly—has the first claim. Exceptions to veracity demand justification, not the other way around. The most obvious exception is matters protected by professional confidentiality, as with information acquired during counseling. Between the extremes of telling all and refusing to tell confidential matters, there are distinctions to be made. To tell some things may well be a breach of confidence even if it is not a matter of explicit professional confidentiality, as, for example, information a friend expects you to keep to yourself. It will always be arguable whether some information may be considered private by nature, being knowledge a prospective employer really has no right to know, or whether honesty requires that it be told. A minister certainly has to consider the effect on pastoral relationships of what he says and writes, even in confidence.

When operating on such difficult ground, ministers should ask a basic question: "Am I hesitant to mention this fact because I am constrained by ethical scruples or because I am not tough-minded enough to tell the truth and face difficult consequences?" The biblical warning, "Woe to you when all persons shall speak well of you" (Luke 6:26) needs to be remembered here; it points to a very natural but often unethical motive for saying nothing but good about others.

If there is competition for a job, one's own candidate may be put at an unfair disadvantage by candor if the recommenders of other candidates are less frank. What is the ethical weight of such a fear?

When a minister feels that there is something that must be told but that would be seriously detrimental to the person, a sound option is to talk to the person, indicate one's view, and ask whether one's name should not be withdrawn as a reference. Even if this is painful, it is more consistent with pastoral caring and responsibility than to gloss the matter.

Useful guidance is to be found in a policy usually followed by church executives among themselves. In recommending ministers for possible posts in other jurisdictions, they follow a high standard of frankness since none wants to be saddled with a problem cleric nor be blamed by another executive for simply unloading a problem. Honesty frequently combines well with self-interest, a union that is an effective motivator. "Recommend unto others as you would have them recommend unto you."

Recommendations are often made in personal conversation or by telephone. If one knows and trusts another, there can be considerable frankness in such communication. This may make for greater honesty. However, we sometimes tell ourselves that we express ourselves better orally, that to put our thoughts in writing seems impersonal and often negative. Such a plea may mask our fear of being held more strictly to account for what we write than for what we say. Do we not assume sometimes that as long as we have not put our judgment in writing we are less likely to be questioned about it? Hypocrisy ever awaits us.

There can be no honesty in communication unless persons asking for letters of reference can assume that evaluations will be honest. There is risk here. It is understood, of course, that a request for recommendation is made to a person holding a basically favorable opinion. If the person asked to respond has serious reservations, the matter should be cleared with the candidate as proposed above.

## Theological Differences between Church Professionals and Lay People

Wide and serious differences in theological outlook between professionals and lay people can make a ministry unworkable. Such differences may erupt in schismatic controversy. The church professional may end up with damage both to ministry and to self, perhaps reaching all the way to the psychiatrist's couch. Some differences always exist and are not in themselves damaging. If handled well, they can enrich congregational life and ministry. Honesty is always an ingredient of this process, even though truth-telling will vary with circumstances.

A first kind of theological difference is simply due to the fact that a professional in ministry has had formal theological education while the people of the church (with few exceptions) have not. This is bound to introduce different ways of understanding Scripture, Christian doctrines, and quite possibly Christian ethics, most notably in regard to social issues. These may appear to be differences in the substance of belief or faith, but are not necessarily that serious. Basic beliefs can be seen in different perspectives. Differences exist in any field between teacher and student or between specialist and nonspecialist. Without them, there would be little need for the church professional's teaching function.

There are, of course, truly substantive differences of belief. It has never been true that all Christians think alike even on basic beliefs, and differences exist within the membership of any congregation. It is impossible for people doing professional ministry to hold the same beliefs as every member. A productive ministry helps a congregation become a forum for constructive discussion of theological issues. Even where there are well-defined denominational standards of correct doctrine, there is need for continuing examination of issues.

Some of these issues lead us to the very foundation of faith. The Bible is authoritative for Christians and supplies the ethical norms for our lives. Yet Scripture has nothing to say directly about such contemporary issues as the despoiling of the natural environment by careless uses of technology or the problems of nuclear warfare or disarmament or what to do about unemployment in a modern economy. Traditional doctrines to which we subscribe may well be expressed in language that is archaic and abstract, so that a recasting in contemporary language is needed in order to enable us to affirm what was intended by the original formula. It is characteristic of faith to seek continually further understanding: *fides quaerens intellectum.* In the process, faith is deepened and people learn to trust a faithful pastor. That is part of what we mean by "growth in grace." As the author of Hebrews says, if we remain on the level of "elementary teaching" we exist on spiritual baby food when we should be ready for solid meat. This growth is not a purely individual matter. We are to grow together into the "fullness of the measure of the stature of Christ." While the teacher has a leading role, it is also true that teachers learn as they teach, both from their students and by means of the teaching itself.

The process by which the minister seeks total truthfulness with the people takes time and rests on a relationship of love and trust. We are familiar with the performance of a minister, fresh from seminary, who

is impelled to confront the people with a whole bagful of avant-garde
ideas, possibly with the notion that this is necessary in order to be
prophetic. Some pastors seem almost to depend on angry reactions to
assure themselves of their integrity. There is more egotism and arrogance
here than Christian love or pastoral caring, much less the recognition
of the requirements of a teaching ministry. When tough issues must be
faced at the risk of hurt feelings, a minister needs a sense of the *kairos*,
the right moment for such matters. At the right time and in the right
way issues can be raised that, far from becoming disruptive, can be
handled so as to enrich the ministry and foster growth in grace.

Having said all this, it remains true that over time the people will
and should come to know where the pastor or church professional stands
on basic theological issues. As with strict avoidance of plagiarism,
ministers must be genuinely themselves in their theological relationships
with their people lest the ties be falsified.

Hypocrisy may come more easily to persons who are apt with words.
We do not denigrate linguistic gifts or skills since language is a great
and distinctively human gift, part of the image of God in us. Ministers
need more, not less of it, even if there are times when actions speak
louder than words and touch or nonverbal symbols communicate more
effectively than words. Still, those practiced in verbalizing must be
careful not to cover their real beliefs with a veil of acceptable words.
Sooner or later we need to be entirely open with our people as to where
we stand. If this should result in a parting of the ways, then it must
be. Truth-telling, even the gentlest and most caring, still has its price.
There is reasonable hope, though, that with Christian love, understanding, and respect, a ministry will be richer and more rewarding for
all differences honestly faced and discussed. How can there be any
teaching or growth unless differences are discovered and openly explored?

### Ordination Vows: "How my mind has changed. . . ."

By "theology" we do not mean primarily technical theological distinctions, although these may well be involved. We are thinking of the
basic beliefs that constitute the content of the faith that the minister
proclaims and teaches. Professing one's theology at ordination is especially characteristic of denominations that have official doctrinal
positions. Even in cases where doctrine is not formalized, however,
there is usually some sense of acceptable theological boundaries. Few
churches, for instance, would accept a minister who proclaimed that
God is dead or who assigned no special role or status to Jesus Christ.

Pastors leave the ministry from time to time owing to loss of faith or conviction. There are many more who do not leave but who are troubled about the fact that they have changed their minds on certain matters. It must be recognized that a time can come when pastors cannot honestly continue to minister in the face of such changes. Integrity demands that they leave the profession. But before that extreme is reached, there are considerations that should be taken into account.

Theology is not revelation: it is not given once-for-all in formulations forever unchangeable. We offer here some distinctions between revelation, faith, and theology. Revelation is God's self-disclosure in redemptive "mighty acts" performed in and through historical events. The normative witness to these acts is the Scripture. "Faith" is our accepting, self-committing response to God. It involves our whole being and determines our basic attitudes, values, and outlook on life. In Karl Barth's phrase, it becomes the "basis of our self-determination." Theology is an effort to understand the content and implications of what is given in revelation and grasped in faith. It is, as we said above, faith seeking understanding. Theology is a human effort at understanding even though it is based on revelation and done in faith. It is revelation that is primarily authoritative, that has a once-for-all quality.[6] Ecclesiastical authority is granted to theological formulations adopted officially by churches. Such authority is not bestowed upon the theologies of either professional theologians or individual believers. Yet in good Reformed fashion we maintain that not only individuals but even councils can err.

Theology is a labor done in a particular historical and cultural context, in a particular time and place. It is right and good that it should be constantly redone, for we need to think through the implications and applications of faith in relation to changing needs, demands, challenges. Some formulations, of course, are believed to hold good beyond such ordinary limits. Most Christian churches subscribe to the Trinitarian formula of Nicaea-Constantinople and the Chalcedonian formula concerning the divinity and humanity of Christ. Reinterpretation of these creeds goes on for the same reasons: culture and history change. Even those who hold that their own beliefs fall within the basic structure and intention of these ancient formulas share in this process.

Every faithful person does theology, for everyone thinks, more or less thoroughly, about that to which she or he is committed in faith. As we live, grow, gain experience, and add knowledge our theology also grows and changes. The inevitability of change can be seen in our development from childhood and youth into adulthood. "When I was a child, I spoke like a child, I thought like a child, I reasoned like a child; when I became a man, I gave up childish ways" (1 Cor. 13:11). Just as we are still the same persons when we become adults, yet different in important ways, so our loyalty to God remains constant, while both our faith and our theology change.

Since ministers are human, their theologies change. The more they maintain the study that is necessary to their profession, the more they can be expected to grow theologically. It should not be assumed that after years of experience, growth, and reflection, one's theology would be the same as at the time of ordination. Change can be for better or worse, but our point is that it is a misunderstanding of theology to assume that it is given once-for-all, static and unchangeable, and that therefore any change must be bad.

A second consideration touches the degree of conviction or certitude that we feel about particular items of belief at any moment. Feelings are notoriously fickle. Aside from sound health maintenance, we do not have a great deal of control over their comings and goings. Yet basic commitments and convictions persist through all the emotional ups and downs. Personal relationships are like this. In the most lasting marriages or friendships there are times when warmth and affection are not at full pitch, times when there are tensions and even temporary alienations. But the relationship survives and emerges stronger when difficulties are worked out honestly. Faith is a living relationship with God that displays some of these characteristics. At any given moment there may be doubts and uncertainties. It is fair to give them time. Honesty does not require that we rush to our ecclesiastical authorities to confess every pulse of doubt as it is felt.

To grant the human spirit space to do its work does not justify posing or pretense. Honesty provides for—indeed, requires—some wrestling over items of belief. In a biblical view, coping with doubt is part of the life of faith. It is crucial to be honest. Martin Buber described the prophets—Jeremiah, for instance—standing before God, "lamenting, complaining to God Himself, disputing with God about justice . . . (We) can speak, (we are) permitted to speak, if only (we) truly speak to God, then there is nothing (we) may not say."[7]

Hypocrisy is not only a matter of deliberately pretending to believe what we do not really hold. It also takes the form of suppressing and refusing to face our doubts, something we may be inclined to do if we view faith as an unfailing certainty. There may also be a problem of guilt involved. Paul Tillich used to tell his students that he had never gotten beyond feeling some guilt each time he advanced an idea which was different from the beliefs he had been taught as a child. In such instances, he said, we should apply the doctrine of justification by faith. Applied to our moral life, it means that God accepts us even though we are unrighteous. Applied to the intellectual side of faith, God accepts us even though we have doubts or experience changes of belief.

Clearly we cannot minister if we no longer believe what we are proclaiming. We tend to fall into routine and become preoccupied with the business of ministry, drifting away from the vision and inspiration that originally launched us into the ministry. As we become more mature we recognize complexities and learn to live without the certainties of youth. If we do not, and instead proceed with the notion that theology should never change and that we should always have absolute certitude, we will resist change, repress actual doubts, and not grow. We never face the question of our changing humanity if we never allow it to arise. If we stop thinking theologically once ordained, we bury whatever talent we have. Those who are actively involved in theological thinking, open to growth and change, sometimes struggling with doubt, are behaving in an ethically responsible way toward their calling to ministry.

## Confidentiality

Confidentiality is a principle that is incorporated into the codes of conduct of several professions. Medical doctors, psychotherapists, and lawyers come to mind immediately. Some recent court cases have debated the position of journalists who feel obligated to protect their sources of information. For the clerical profession, the prototype is no doubt the Roman Catholic confessional, where confidentiality is absolute and is defended uncompromisingly.

Confidentiality has both legal and ethical dimensions. In the famous Tarasoff case,[8] a young man confided to his psychologist (who was employed by a university hospital) that he intended to kill a young woman. Members of the psychiatric staff conferred, decided that the man should be committed for observation, and requested the assistance of the police. The police talked to the man, judged him rational, and released him. The head of the psychiatric department then decreed that no further action be taken. Shortly thereafter, the young man killed the woman. In the lawsuit that the parents brought against the authorities involved, the defense argued that the principle of confidentiality justified the failure to disclose. On a narrow 5–4 decision, the state court rejected this argument and decided against the defendants. A strong dissenting minority, however, held that the confidentiality principle was valid and must be observed absolutely or it would not work at all. It was argued further that greater good results in the long run if the principle is upheld, despite harm that may result in some cases. The minority argued, like Kant, for an absolute rule backed up by appeal to social utility and long-range good consequences.

Confidentiality has another dimension in the case of the Roman Catholic confessional. Even the worst of criminals must have a chance to confess sins to God, even if they are never confessed to human authorities. This consideration overrides all others, requiring absolute confidentiality on the part of the priest as the human mediator of the confession. He can urge the guilty party to turn himself in and make amends but cannot reveal the facts. To the present time, the laws of the states and decisions of courts have respected this "religious" confidentiality. But problems exist both for legal authorities and for the conscience of the priest. Suppose, as happens, that someone is being tried or is already being punished for a crime for which another person has admitted responsibility in the confessional. Does not responsibility require some way of making exceptions to the confidentiality even of the confessional?

It is fortunate that such situations do not occur as often as might be suggested by dramatizations of them on television. As far as the law is concerned, the problem for clergy may not be to protect confidentiality against the demands of police or courts but rather to cope with malpractice suits if confidentiality is not maintained. There have already been a few suits against clergy on the same sorts of grounds that apply to any counselor, such as giving advice to a couple that they believe to have harmed them. One may hope that church professionals will not become involved with lawsuits and malpractice insurance on the scale of the medical profession.

Protestant ministers are constrained by confidentiality, just as are Roman Catholic priests. Protestants believe, of course, that confession can be made by the individual directly to God without a priestly mediator. Yet a human confessor can be helpful and in many counseling situations the minister does function as confessor in a way necessary to the counseling process.

How are exceptions to the obligation of confidentiality to be decided?

Any ethical principle must be held subject to exception in unusual or extraordinary situations. Exceptions occur when two rules, ordinarily compatible, come into conflict, so that we must decide which should be granted priority. Both rules remain valid in themselves; the exception remains an exception. Unless we accept this, we shall confront difficulties like those of Kant's unexceptionable rule of truth-telling.

We hold that where the possibility of serious harm or grave injustice to another is at stake the rule of confidentiality is subject to exception. The objection to this is that unless confidentiality is made absolute, no one will trust the counselor or confessor and the counseling process itself will be undermined. We question whether this necessarily follows. People are not incapable of understanding the reasons for making exceptions. We suspect that in practice most people side with Bonhoeffer rather than with Kant on the truth-telling issue. It is true that confidentiality suffers some impairment when an exception is made. But there is greater loss if confidentiality is maintained at the price of human life, as when a homicidally inclined counselee carries out a threat to kill someone. The defenders of absolute confidentiality hold, implicitly or explicitly, that the loss involved in the breaking of confidentiality will always outweigh losses entailed by maintaining it. But there is no factual evidence that enables us to make such a judgment for all possible situations. Exceptions are not easy to decide. They must be decided on the merits of each particular case and honest differences of judgment must be allowed.

There are many situations in which conflicts of responsibility arise. They are somewhat more easily resolved in favor of strict confidentiality because the consequences for others are not quite so severe. Yet they can be serious. In the case of the teenage girl involved with an older man described in the example at the outset of chapter 1, the pastor has obligations to the parents, who are parishioners, as well as to the girl. If this older man is married, the minister's obligations extend even to the man's wife and to his children, if any. If the teenager is a minor, an issue of statutory rape may exist, depending on local law. Furthermore, the girl could become involved most unpleasantly in a suit for divorce.

Parents left uninformed while such difficulties grow ever more serious have reason to complain of a minister who would keep them ignorant of what so deeply concerns them. A minister might be justly accused of misjudgment and unprofessionalism in failing to bring them into the matter before it comes to a head. There is the likelihood that the affair will become known at a time and in a way that will increase its painfulness to all concerned. The parents' confidence in the pastor will certainly diminish and lasting damage may be done to the bonds of the parents and their daughter.

Obviously the pastor will make every effort to persuade the girl to take her parents into her confidence, all the more imperative if she is a minor. In addition to the obvious personal reasons for this, professionals have an obligation to the law—in this case, the responsibility of parents for the behavior of their minor children.

If the young counselee refuses to share her problem with her parents, her purpose in seeking counsel becomes crucial. Is she seeking help in terminating the affair? If she is prepared to take steps promptly to put it behind her, a pastor may rightly assure her that confidentiality will be maintained without exception. There are sound reasons for defending such a decision, even though parents may feel they had a right to know. It may be that confidential counsel was essential to success in bringing the affair to resolution.

If the teenager has not come for help in terminating the affair, the problem is more difficult. Why did she come? To boast? To find out how to deal with its impending disclosure? Because she is pregnant? It is impossible to spell out all the courses of action that follow from each of these. Suffice it to say that ethically responsible decisions on any aspect of counselling in a situation such as this depend on keeping the main purpose of the counseling clearly in view: in this case, to restore this young woman to a style of life compatible with Christian teaching and to effect justice for all persons injured by her behavior. The minister should bend toward maintenance of confidentiality, not toward finding grounds for an exception. The resolution of the problem rather than the counselor's own defense against anticipated criticism should remain central. The most substantial reason for an exception to confidentiality would be where that exception promised substantial assistance in helping the teenager make a new beginning. While the pain inflicted on parents by the girl's behavior and possibly by the minister's decision to respect confidentiality is real, it is not so serious as in other cases where a threat to life or the languishing in prison of someone who is not guilty of a crime are involved. A pastor is in position to help the parents see why confidentiality was maintained and to understand that their daughter would not have come for help apart from that assurance.

In many cases in which confidentiality is proper there may be recriminations if the facts become known through some other avenue.

*Pastor T. is counseling with a married man, a member of the congregation, together with his wife. It turns out that the man is having an affair with another woman, also a member of the congregation. In what seems genuine repentance, the man breaks off the affair. His wife has not known of this. Should she be told? The husband decides not to do so and Pastor T. feels bound by confidentiality to go along. Unfortunately, the rejected woman reveals the affair. The wife, hurt and angry, feels betrayed by the pastor as well as her husband and leaves the congregation.*

The outcome of such experiences does not prove the pastor's decisions wrong. Pastor T. paid a price for her decision, but it was the best of the options open to her. Through pastoral caring and counsel, perhaps by another pastor, the injured wife can be helped to see that confidentiality was necessary. Further, this counsel can possibly help her to receive back an honestly repentant husband and seek a reconstructed marriage. Where such efforts do not succeed, consequences must simply be accepted.

It is important to include in a church education program means by which pastor or church professionals and people can discuss confidentiality as part of pastoral ministry. Laity may not realize what is involved in professional ethics. To understand professional ethical dilemmas before they themselves are touched by such decisions as the above helps to achieve constructive outcomes to situations where principles conflict.

When expectations of confidentiality are not made explicit, situations may arise in which one party does not realize what is expected and lets the secret out. If a minister is the one who talks, the act may appear as a breach of trust. If one is working in a counseling or confessional context, the requirement of confidentiality is clear. In casual conversations it may not be so apparent. Ministers should be especially aware of the risks here and if there is any room for doubt, keep the matter in confidence.

Clergy have said of themselves that as a group they may have a more than average inclination to gossip. While we have no scientific studies to confirm this, personalities who are attracted to this profession enjoy human contact and are often ready talkers. Chatty conversation may easily drift into gossip. Genuine interest in other human beings may cause us to talk gratuitously about other persons with no harm intended. An added danger is that originally harmless remarks may be misquoted or quoted out of context and become damaging. Insofar as all this may be true of ministers, they need to be doubly discreet.

Drinkers who are candid with themselves know very well that alcohol improves neither judgment nor discretion and fuels the wagging tongue. When normal constraints on emotion are relaxed, impulses control behavior much more easily, including the impulse to talk too loudly, too long, and too much. If there is a professional ethic of alcohol consumption, its necessity and content arise from the abundance of unprofessional behaviors associated with it. In a word, who wants a lush for a pastor?

Pastors are persistently tempted to use counseling cases as illustrations in sermons. Usually an effort is made to doctor the circumstances to avoid identification of the persons involved. It sometimes happens that the identities are guessed, or the parties involved may recognize the story and feel the risk of disclosure should not have been taken. Sermons do need to be informed by the practical experiences of the preacher. They are enriched by the interplay between faith and theology on the one hand and lived experience on the other. We suggest, however, that unless one is very clever at "doctoring," illustrative examples should be drawn from experience in other communities, published professional books and journals, realistic situations in good novels, or even other people's sermons (with the source mentioned!). It is wise to exercise caution in such matters.

In this chapter we have touched five of the dilemmas faced by almost all church professionals. The problems associated with truth spread to the furthest reaches of professional activity. We have remarked earlier that there are two poles to truth-telling: the truth itself and the person as truth-teller in a living human situation. The truth has authority; it imposes itself upon us. Do those who are called to proclaim and interpret the truth also have authority in some sense? What is the nature of this call? We shall consider this question before dealing with further ethical problems encountered in the professional practice of ministry.

# PART TWO
# AUTHORITY

# 3

## The Authority
## of the Minister

People who believe that God has granted them knowledge of truth and who furthermore believe it to be a personal duty to tell that truth to others harbor a conviction of personal authority, whether they recognize it or not. One cannot imagine the most revered teachers of the church—St. Paul, St. Augustine, Luther, or Calvin—without the opinion that they both knew and had the authority to tell the truth.

On the other hand, the world is awash with religious assertiveness, often accompanied by ambitions and behaviors very different from the life of poverty and service taught by Jesus and the apostles. To be both an honest and forthright spokesperson for the Word of God and a humble servant of all people is not easy. Ethical integrity rests on a theologically sound and workable solution to the dichotomies of authority and service, of confidence and humility, of the strong selfhood of the prophet and the self-effacement of one called to serve others.

### Temptations to Egoism

Some examples may help to clarify this issue.

*A Presbyterian elder returned from a session meeting very angry. "What's the matter?" asked her husband. "Oh, that minister of ours!" she replied. "He's great in many ways: a conscientious pastor who really cares about people, hard-working, a good preacher, and he certainly has built up the membership. But he's a dictator! Under his smooth manner he runs things to suit himself. He always gets his*

*way. Tonight we were supposed to discuss his proposal for a $20,000
renovation on the large meeting room. Some of us thought the money
might be better spent in other ways but when the subject came up he
just overrode all objections, closed the discussion, and called for a
vote. He had lined up a hard core of support before the meeting and
most of the others went along because they like him and don't want a
fuss. That man trades on the affection of the people! The more able
and successful ministers are the more autocratic they become."*

The question of a minister's authority may come up much more subtly
and personally in other circumstances.

*A minister had just returned from calling on a new family in the
community and had invited them to consider joining the congregation.
They had indicated that they were drawn to another church but
promised to consider the matter further. The conversation had
convinced the minister that the couple was more conservative than
most of her own members. "And yet," she reflected, "we need to be
open to Christians of different persuasions. That's the way a church
should be. Our congregation would be better for having them." As
she turned the matter over in her mind, the minister recognized a
motive that was deeply personal: she prided herself on being able to
minister to all sorts of different personalities. "I feel defeated if I lose
a member," she admitted to herself, "especially if another minister
seems better able to meet that person's need than I."*

*A few days later she attended a meeting where she lunched with a
friend and fellow pastor. She told him her thoughts about the visit. "I
understand your problem," he replied. "But don't we have to
counteract the tendency of American Protestantism to build
congregations around the personalities and opinions of particular
ministers?" "That's a danger," she answered. "You know, my desire
to minister to many kinds of people may be connected with the 'myth
of omnicompetence' we discussed at the ministerial association
recently. Maybe I've just got a big ego! I remember being disturbed
by the interview for my present job. The committee said that the
congregation expected their pastor to provide all the elements of
ministry equally well: preaching, teaching, counseling, administration,
and all the rest. I have a general competence but I know very well
that I do some things better than others."*

*"Although we know better," said her companion, "we may begin
to believe that myth. Sometimes I get really wound up in preaching. I*

*feel as though the Word were really coming through. I feel like a real prophet. Then I get to wondering if I have confused my own words with God's Word."*

In the first of the above examples the successful minister was apparently working from a view of clerical authority that left him quite untroubled by the impression of high-handedness made on some lay people. The pastor in the second example was honestly struggling for self-assurance.

An almost infinite range of examples may be cited touching the polarity of dominance and humility, confidence and modesty. Both the pastors in the above cases had concepts of how a minister ought to behave and perhaps very sound ideas about the ministry itself. Yet the balance of being able to act with assurance without being arrogant was lacking. To have this assurance, a stable understanding of the meaning of the profession must undergird daily work.

The authors have been impressed by the number of pastors who have mentioned that the expectations of the congregation pose a problem for them. Both the general impressions of people about what ministers ought to be and the job descriptions formulated by pastoral search committees reveal a rather idealistic and perfectionistic concept of the minister. Pastors are expected to be "all things to all people." Aside from the desire of the congregations to have a minister who will never pass forty-five, always increase membership and budget year-by-year, demonstrate ability to attract young people, always maintain a pleasing manner and attractive appearance, there are the inescapable demands for skill in public speaking, counseling, teaching, administration, and all the rest—not to mention honest piety and sincere morality (however these may be understood). Obviously, congregations settle for a good deal less than all this in actual cases, yet pastors with an eye to a future call are aware of these expectations and know they will be in competition with other candidates.

Here we are back to a question of honesty and truth-telling. We must be clear and honest about our concept of ministry and what normative expectations we have. Christian theology allows room for what ought ideally to be and also for what may, in reality, be expected. Laity have an instinct for this. They do not really expect perfection. Yet they too have assumptions that form their concept of ministry.

## The Meaning of Ministry

Today Protestant, Roman Catholic, and Eastern Orthodox concepts of ministry show broad agreement. Our intention here is ecumenical even if some readers may detect our own Reformed theological slip showing a bit.

A first point of agreement is that ministry is for all Christians; all are to participate. The ministry precedes and transcends all distinctions between clergy and laity. The Roman Catholic theologian Edward Schillebeeckx recently made this point as forcefully as one can.[1] He notes that two concepts of ministry have arisen in the church's history. According to the earlier concept, the ministry belongs to the whole church; all members have a part in it. But not everyone has the same part, since the ministry is diversified. The various types of ministry are based on different spiritual gifts, *charismata*, bestowed by the Holy Spirit.[2] Included in this variety are *charismata* given to some to enable them to perform leading and presiding functions. The community selects and ordains to clerical ministry members who appear to have such gifts. The liturgy of ordination and the laying on of hands in particular symbolize that it is the church as a whole that ordains, and that ordained ministry is part of the ministry of the whole church. The ordination prayer with its *epiclesis* (calling upon the Spirit) recognizes that it is the Spirit who validates and empowers the ministry. What happens in the *ecclesia* is a gift of God's Spirit and not an expression of the autonomy of the church. The movement is from Spirit through church to minister.[3]

The second view, which in time became dominant in the Roman Catholic church, according to Schillebeeckx, holds that the priest receives "sacred power" (*sacra potestas*) at ordination. This power is attached especially to the sacraments, which are *signa efficax gratiae* (symbols that effect grace).

Any Christian doctrine of ministry is christologically based.[4] However, the second view "gave the ministry a directly christological basis and shifted the mediation of the church into the background"—and with it, emphasis on the Spirit. The "sacred power" is treated as though it were "the priest's personal possession. In this way the ecclesial significance of the ministry with its charismatic and pneumatological dimensions is obscured and the more time goes on, the more the ministry is embedded in a legalistic cadre which bestows sacred power."[5]

The first view is found in the New Testament where "it is Christ and the church who are priestly; nowhere in the New Testament does the minister in the church take on particularly priestly characteristics."[6] The ancient distinction between *klerikos* and *laikos* should be taken to refer only to different types of ministry, not to a difference of "status." It does not suggest a distinction between super- and subordination, *praelatio* and *subiectio*. All ministries are forms of service for which individuals are equipped by gifts of the Spirit. Ordained ministry is appropriate for those who are gifted for "the service of leading the community." But the *charismata*, not the formality of ordination, are the primary reason for this role in the community. Schillebeeckx believes that persons with these gifts may appear in any local assemblage of Christians. He suggests that where there is a shortage of priests some of these unordained persons who already have all of the essential requirements for the ministry of leadership might well be appointed to that ministry. He mentions specifically "many catechists in Africa, and men and women pastoral workers in Europe and elsewhere."[7]

There are many persons in all denominations who agree on the following points: God constitutes ministry in the world following the life of Christ by calling a people to serve. Ministry therefore is first of all the ministry of the whole church. Ordained ministry is part of this larger, diverse ministry. All forms of ministry are of equal honor and status.

The second point on which there is general agreement is that ministry means serving. The model is Christ, who was and is the Suffering Servant. The Christ who is for others—indeed, the whole *agape*-based ethic of the New Testament—obviously leaves no room for dominating or domineering attitudes among clergy. If ordained ministers lead, they lead in a ministry of serving.

> You know that those who are supposed to rule over the Gentiles lord it over them, and their great men exercise authority over them. But it shall not be so among you; but whoever would be great among you must be your servant, and whoever would be first among you must be slave of all. For the Son of man also came not to be served but to serve, and to give his life as a ransom for many.[8]

Whatever else we may say about the authority that is appropriate to ordained ministry, it cannot be understood so as to contradict this basic point.

The service of believers cannot be confined to serving each other within the church. It takes place in the world that God loves and for which Christ died. What we often treat as a kind of addendum to faith and ministry and call "social action" is an integral part of ministry properly understood.[9]

Karl Barth (who can hardly be accused of advocating a liberal social gospel) says forcefully of the church that it

> builds up itself and its members in the common hearing of the Word of God which is always new in common prayer, in Baptism, and the Lord's

61

Supper, in the practice of its inner fellowship, in theology. But it cannot forget that it cannot do these things simply for its own sake but only in the course of its commission, only in an implicit and explicit outward movement to the world with which Jesus Christ and, in his person, God accepted solidarity, for which he died and in which he rose again. . . . In its deepest and most proper tendency, the Church is not churchly but worldly, the Church with open doors and great windows, behind which it does better not to close itself in upon itself again, by putting in pious stained-glass windows. It is holy in its openness to the street and even the alley, in its turning to the profanity of all human life, the holiness which, according to Rom. 12:15 does not scorn to rejoice with them that rejoice and weep with them that weep.[10]

In Barth's view the scope of reconciliation and redemption is the whole creation, not just the church. God is already working in the world in all its secularity. Christ's ministry and mission have always been in the world. While the church cannot save the world by its efforts (only God can do that), still our ministry is the part we are called to play within the whole saving action of God in the world. However we may see our social responsibilities in regard to particular issues, we cannot conceive that the church or religion are ends in themselves. They cannot be defined or served apart from the world and its secular politics, economics, and other social systems.

Authority necessary and appropriate to ordained ministry is the third point of agreement among Christians. This office of the church's ministry involves particular responsibilities that must be exercised with integrity, forthrightness, and courage. This is grounded in the New Testament. The passage quoted above from Matthew and Mark about serving others rather than ruling them occurs in a slightly different form in Luke 22:24-27. In the first two Gospels the setting is the period when Jesus begins his final journey to Jerusalem. In the Gospel of Mark, James and John (in Matthew's Gospel, their mother) ask Jesus to grant them places of honor beside him when the kingdom comes. In Luke, however, the setting is the Last Supper. The occasion is a dispute among all the disciples about which of them is the greatest.[11] The Last Supper is also the setting for an incident in John's Gospel that we regularly link with the others, namely, the foot-washing episode. The main point of this passage has to do with Judas' betrayal of Jesus[12] but it also includes two points that are directly pertinent to our discussion. First, Jesus is humble and washes his disciples' feet; therefore, the disciples should do likewise—be humble and serve each other. But there is a note of authority here: "You call me Teacher and Lord; and you are right, for so I am. If I, then, your Lord and Teacher, have washed your feet, you also ought to wash one another's feet. For I have given you an example."[13]

In declarations issued by churches it is regularly stated that the ministry in our time is to be modelled on that of Jesus himself. While Jesus is more than our example and our ministry is a participation in his continuing ministry, he is still not less than our example.[14] We do not claim the full authority of Jesus himself or pretend to the selfless purity of his loving service of others; nevertheless, we find in Jesus our model for ministry. Despite his rejection of "lording it over" others, of both authoritarian and autocratic behavior, Jesus' model of humble servant has a streak of irony in it. The Gospel accounts portray him as excoriating hypocrites and confronting people with the truth about God and themselves.

The authority of the clergy is not its own; it is Christ's and is conveyed by the gospel entrusted to the church. Still, our responsibility is to take care that this truth is neither sacrificed nor compromised. It must be proclaimed both in its original form, Scripture, and its appropriate forms in contemporary situations. This is where grit is sometimes needed. Ministry is humble and loving but it also requires courage, even stubbornness, and a capacity for plain speaking. The humble servant of the Word is no wishy-washy Charlie Brown.

## The Minister as Teacher: The "Watching Brief"

Power and authority belong first to God, incarnate in Christ and present by the Spirit. It also belongs to the Word about what God has done and is doing and this Word we are to proclaim. There is, as it were, a spillover of authority which comes through Christ to us in ministry. T. F. Torrance suggests that while Christ is the only priest and always the supreme authority, "permanent elements of significance" in that priesthood may be carried over and "transferred from Christ" implicitly in ordination.[15]

Torrance upholds ordained ministry as primarily a ministry of preaching and administering sacraments but sees authority as connected also with teaching. The laying on of hands commissions us to "proclaim the kerygma and teach the didache." He goes on to mention the historical role of "doctors" (teachers) of the church, who are ministers with "a special charisma for teaching doctrine and for keeping a 'watching brief' over the purity of the church's proclamation and doctrine in obedience to the teaching of the apostles."

We here use "teaching" to indicate a special responsibility of ordained ministers that carries with it a particular kind of authority. As we use the term, it refers to a dimension of the ministry as a whole and not only to such specific activities as teaching communicants classes, adult education courses, and the like. John Calvin usually distinguished between ministries of teaching and preaching but he also said that the same person might perform both and in one passage actually merged the two.[16] In local congregations the pastor, being specially trained theologically and with particular responsibility for the Word (in both preaching and sacramental celebration) is the one who has the authority of the watching brief over the whole life and ministry of the church. The watching brief pertains only to the special role of the ordained minister in the ministry of the whole church. That is, the pastor has a special (though not exclusive) responsibility to see that the congregation stays on track, to be sure that what it does is consistent with the gospel and is fitting for the body of Christ taking shape in the world. The watching brief calls for nurturing the congregation toward understanding its faith and calling. It may also call for "whistle blowing" if things go off the track.

The watching brief is the pastor's special responsibility. This does not set ordained ministers above others except in this single respect. Their authority is never greater than the status or authority of other types of ministry in respect to their own particular contributions. As Barth says, every one of the ministries of the church has its own "eminence and responsibility." None has the right to make autonomous demands or claims or expect to be accorded special dignities or privileges. Each ministerial authority is justified only as it contributes to the requirement of service under which the church stands. Nevertheless, there are legitimate demands that may be made by one part of the church upon the whole if such is "necessary to fulfill the common requirement of service."[17]

## The Application of Authority

With these biblical and theological understandings of a minister's authority before us, how is it to be exercised in parish life or in other kinds of pastoral ministry?

Karl Barth has proposed three meanings of the Word of God, which he sees as the basis of the very existence of the church and of the "authority" that any within it might claim: (1) the Word as Jesus Christ, the embodiment of the self-expression (logos) of God in human history; (2) the Word as Scripture, the basic witness to "God's mighty acts"; (3) and the Word proclaimed, which refers to that work of the Holy Spirit by which Christ is made present and real for us in the whole life and ministry of the church.[18] Word means that not only preaching but sacraments, or the Word enacted, are fundamental to the whole ministry. It also includes our encountering and knowing Christ in responsible relationship to neighbors both inside and outside the church. Authority resides in Christ and the scriptural witness, and the church's ministry and proclamation are subject to evaluation and criticism in their light.[19]

The pastor has everything to do with these manifestations of the Word. They are given first to the church as a whole, but pastors have a special responsibility for the watching brief. While the clergy does not constitute a body charged to supervise morals, no pastor can accept a damaging betrayal of the witness and life of the Word in the congregation without taking action. Responsibility for the integrity of the Word demands protest when the Word is brought into disrepute. Lay officers of the church have a similar obligation, especially where clergy misconduct may be concerned. The warrant for such judgment comes from the fulfillment of roles in ministry, not a superior moral position.

In the second manifestation of the Word, Scripture, the pastor is its teacher and bears the authority and responsibility conferred at ordination both to teach effectively and to see that it is taught faithfully throughout the programs and activities of the church. If a particular individual attempts to convert a church school class, for example, into a personal forum rather than a place for the teaching of the Word, the minister cannot refrain from intervention. For the role of teacher, a pastor is prepared by thorough biblical and theological education.

In the manifestation of the Word as proclaimed, the pastor bears authority and responsibility for clear preaching and solemn enactment of the Word in sacramental celebration. Pastors should not be guilty of ill-prepared sermons nor tolerant of fellow professionals who indulge in slipshod performance, whether they are members of the same staff in a local ministry or participants in the same denominational ministry.

A certain practical authority arises in consequence of a thorough theological education. Christians do not claim authority on the basis of academic degrees; they know that it arises solely in the Christ who is their life and Word. But church professionals have examined the life and teachings of Christ, the text of the Bible, and the history of the church and they have studied the ways in which revelation is understood by the ablest Christian thinkers. If this scholarly grounding is strong, the clergy is entitled to personal respect and the practical authority implied by sound learning. Lay members also have special competences, sometimes in theological disciplines, and enjoy the consequent practical authority. The laity often have insights of faith that generate significant theology. For example, Latin American liberation theologians credit the laity in the Christian "base communities" of Latin America with having laid the foundations for this theology. Theologians must be willing to learn from laity. Nevertheless, clerics have a formal responsibility for the essentially theological task of keeping the practice of the church consistent with the Word.

## Temptations to False Humility: Dodging Responsibility

With all that has been said about ways in which clerics fall victim to egoistic temptations, there are equally serious dangers on the opposite side. Speaking with authority is sometimes both right and necessary and to do otherwise is simply to duck responsibility and so to fail morally and professionally. We have heard ministers express misgivings about "professionalism," feeling that the use of the word amounts to a pretense to elitism. Yet these same people may fail to speak with authority when their special role should come into play. Or, if they are naturally dominant, their manner of exercising authority may lack the self-discipline that is intrinsic to true professionalism.

A common failure of clergy is to permit study and reflection to be swept aside by the torrent of daily claims on their time. Theological education is not timeless, not because truth erodes but because the mind forgets, new experiences need to be thought through on the basis of earlier learning, and techniques and required competencies change. Is it true humility in a professional to allow the pressures of daily work to weaken the foundations? Are not professions of humble service likely to become excuses for simple failure to impose discipline on the use of time and the pressures of work?

Professor Joseph Sittler has spoken to a commonplace of pastoral experience:

> Someone ought to speak up against what I call the maceration of the minister. . . . The minister's time, his [sic] focussed sense of vocation, his vision of his central task, his mental life, and his contemplative acreage—they are all under the chopper. . . . What the (theological) schools elevate, the actual practice of ministry flattens. The schools urge to competence in various fields of theological study. The canons of competence that

determine the churches' practice . . . are radically destructive of (the schools') precedence and nurture. . . . His teachers were concerned that he not become so insensible as to make such easy identifications with the Kingdom of God as characterize the promotional literature of our . . . churches. Visit the (former student) some years later in what he still calls inexactly his "study" and one is more likely to find him accompanied by the same volumes he took with him from his student room. And filed on top of these are mementoes of what he is presently concerned with: a roll of blueprints, a file of negotiations between the parish, the bank, and the Board of Missions; samples of asphalt tile and a plumber's estimate. When one wonders what holds the man together, enables him to bring equal enthusiasm to his practical decisions and his pastoral and proclamatory function, one learns that he is held together—if he is—by his public role of responsibility for the external advancement of the congregation. . . . Studies become less and less an occupation intrinsic to his role as witness to the gospel and pastor to people and become more and more frantic efforts to find biblical or theological generalities which will religiously dignify his promotional purposes. The will of God has got to be simplified into a push for the parish house. The Holy Spirit is reduced to a holy resource which can be used as a punch line for the enforcement of parish purposes. [20]

Theological competence in ministry means not only having theological knowledge but also having the skill to think theologically about what one is doing. Professor Sittler, in the above quotation, expressed grave doubt about how much competence is found in ministerial practice. His assessment may be unfair. Some of the blame may be laid upon church members who place theological study and reflection low on the scale of what they assume they are paying their pastors to do. The problem is largely rooted in the situation of the pastor. Pastors are besieged by an overwhelming number of demands and the more practical ones always seem more clamant. Programs have to be organized by a certain time. Budgets have deadlines. Cases of illness, crisis situations, death and dying must be dealt with now. Committee meetings will occur as scheduled. Time and energy are consumed and little of either is left for more long-range matters such as theological study and reflection.

To paraphrase Immanuel Kant, the truth is that while thinking without doing is empty, doing without thinking is blind. What does it profit us if we fill our barns with activity while our souls go unfed? The very pressures we have recognized make it all the more necessary to take time to think theologically about what we are doing. The constant evaluation of one's work that is intrinsic to truly professional quality work requires established habits of theological reflection which are hard to acquire without continual theological reading. When clerics fail to do this they let down the church and default on a moral obligation. Claims to humble service may obscure mere weakness or an inadequate inner sense of authority in the pastor's role.

There are real difficulties in preserving time for study. Many pastors accept responsibility for failure to study, confessing that they really do not have a valid excuse. It takes a confident sense of professional selfhood to set aside time for study and to defend it. We tend to treat study time as essentially unassigned and therefore available for other purposes rather than constituting a prior commitment. Some pastors may unconsciously shy away from reading and study. Involvement in continuing education programs, degree or nondegree, is one way to help oneself. As two critics of their own profession have suggested,[21] one of the reasons for what they see as failure to maintain standards of excellence in the practice of law has been the tendency to assume that once one has earned a degree and passed bar exams, one is forever qualified to practice. An analogous assumption is not unfamiliar among clerics.

Clergy sometimes dodge responsibility by invoking the blessed role of peacemaker. It is sometimes forgotten that if Jesus said "Blessed are the peacemakers. . . ." he also said: "I came to cast fire on the earth . . ." and "I have not come to bring peace, but a sword. . . ."[22] A lot of clerical peacemaking obscures a failure to understand the rightful authority of the minister or a reluctance to take the risk of exercising it, as the following vignette exemplifies.

> A minister's denomination had taken a stand urging negotiation for a halt in nuclear arms production as part of a lengthy program of active peacemaking. Pastors were urged to preach on the theme. The minister wanted to comply but was fearful of angry reactions from many of her members who would see such policy proposals as dangerous to the nation's security and perhaps even question her patriotism. The minister was fearful lest such reactions split the congregation or at least alienate important members. On a later Sunday morning, therefore, the minister brought forth her solution. She announced at the worship service that she was going to preach on the topic of peace, as recommended by her denomination. In the Bible, she pointed out, the word "peace" has many meanings. The specific topic of her choice was "peace within"! There was not a word about the reconciliation of nations in conflict. So the peace of the congregation was preserved.

Among clergy there is a certain pride in the image of peacemaker. As one participant in a discussion remarked: "I don't know that we are any more likely to compromise our convictions under pressure than anybody else, but maybe one form of that particular temptation does have something to do with the image of the minister as peacemaker. I am thinking of our training in counseling. We have gotten leery of being overly directive. We'd rather serve by helping and healing than by challenging. Is that so bad?"

Our problem here may be a mistaken idea of humility. Martin Marty has been quoted as saying that clergy are not usually guilty of really serious misdeeds but their vices grow out of their virtues.[23] The first virtue mentioned is humility. The writer of the article citing Marty suggested that too much humility, or humility misunderstood, can easily amount to an inadequate sense of personal worth and a failure to affirm the dignity of the profession. He observed that some clergy fall into the habit of "poor-mouthing" their profession.

Situations such as these pose some troubling questions that take us to the root of the matter—what it means to be a minister. Lacking a clear understanding of both the church's ministry and the ordained ministry, no pastor is able to think through the ambiguities of daily work with a view to acting ethically. Because the purpose of this book is precisely to help clergy think and act ethically, it is now necessary for us to present our view of the ministry as a profession. With these perspectives clarified—and in hope of furnishing our readers with strengthened understandings fundamental to thinking theologically about ethical issues—we will then return to ethical analysis of cases.

# 4

# The Pastor
# as Professional

The term "professional" has negative implications for some people but no other serves as well to situate authority in its proper context. The authority of doctors, lawyers, pastors, and other professionals is not innate, as though they were born into a social aristocracy, nor is authority a perquisite of genius. It requires a rational ground. Professional authority finds its ground in high qualification.

The professional lives in a balance between two sensibilities. One is the confidence that arises from thorough education, sound theoretical understanding, and an experience of successful application of knowledge through technical skill. The other is an awareness of personal limitations that prevents errors in judgment that would harm patients, clients, or counselees. This practical balance is analogous to the theological balance between authority grounded in Christ the Word and the obligation to serve in all humility.

The concern of the pastor in our lengthy example in the previous chapter concerning the myth of omnicompetence was by no means unprofessional. Professional self-understanding includes idealistic components—for example, a commitment to be all things to all people, with St. Paul—and yet is always accompanied by the awareness that no person can altogether surmount individual limitations. The power of the gospel transcends all human particularities but does not empower all ministers equally. St. Paul can best minister to some, Apollos to others, and Cephas to still others. Christ alone ministers to all—yet he remains the primary model of the minister. The pastor in our example would have been wholly justified in saying to the conservative folk she had visited: "Go to Rev. Apollos' church; I think the ministry of that congregation will meet your needs better than ours."

## The Professional Idea

Both the definition and the nature of the professions and the roles and responsibilities of professionals have changed in the course of Western history.[1] In the Middle Ages professions developed under the aegis of the church; all professionals (priest, teacher, lawyer, physician, civil servant) were clerics. Professionals then were intellectuals mainly interested in theory, however. Most of the practical work was done by subprofessional groups, many of them constituting guilds. Grocers served as apothecaries, surgery was done by barbers. "Common" lawyers and notaries did much of the legal work. By about 1600 all professions except clergy had become secular. Those chiefly recognized were ministry, medicine, and law. Their members were by that time jfrom the upper classes with university educations. Their chief interests and activities remained intellectual and theoretical. During the nineteenth century, with the advance of science and technology, technical competence gradually became the primary criterion of professions and theoretical competencies were conjoined with the more practical skills of the subprofessional guilds in the new professional organizations.

In many nations during the twentieth century, the number of the professions has expanded with many new occupations seeking recognition as professions. This has necessitated efforts to establish criteria by which a profession can be defined and identified. With the proliferation of knowledge and specialized practice there has also been a growing need to define and maintain standards of competence and practice.

Ministry has always been considered one of the professions, if only because of the clerical origins of professions in our culture. It is both like and unlike other professions, especially those of medicine and law, with which it is often compared. It is (or should be) most like these other professions in regard to its teaching function; here a sense of being professional is important to the clergy. However, there are aspects of a certain professionalism that distorts true ministry. Both positive and negative considerations help us to clarify the meaning of authority in ministry.

The following characteristics are commonly used to define a true profession:

—It renders a specialized service to persons in society which meets a complex need and on which society places a high value.

—It possesses and uses specialized knowledge essential to this service, knowledge of two sorts: a body of relevant theory, and proficiency in certain practical techniques or skills—the "know-how" of the profession.

—Its members accept moral responsibility in at least three respects: their commitment to high standards of performance in practice involving integrity, competence, and excellence; the motive of service, which for them is primary, especially in contrast to material gain or social status; and commitment to honorable relations with fellow professionals.

—It is organized in a professional society that helps to define standards for and has a role in admission to practice,[2] promotes and supervises continuing application of standards of performance and service, and protects and promotes the ethically justifiable interests of its members.

These criteria favor the classical professions such as law and medicine and would probably exclude many occupations that are striving for recognition as professions today. The requirement of theoretical knowledge, for example, best fits professions that demand both an undergraduate degree and training in a graduate professional school. It is useful to select for comparison those professions that most nearly resemble the ministry.

To contrast the word professional with amateur can be misleading. When contrasted with "amateur," Dr. James Glasse suggests, "professional" means skilled, full-time, and paid whereas "amateur" means less skilled, part-time, and unpaid. With the roles of clergy and laity, we have argued that ministries of the church performed by lay people are no less important and require no less skill than those performed by clergy. Another distinction Glasse notes suggests that amateurs perform out of pure love for what they do (as in sports, traditionally) while professionals are motivated by the pay they receive. This distorts the motivation of the best professionals and denies the consistent emphasis in the ethics of all professions upon service as motive rather than desire for material gain. Professionals enter their occupations because they enjoy doing what they do and find fulfillment in it.[3]

## The Centrality of Theological Competence

We are particularly concerned with the application to ministry of the second and third criteria of professions mentioned above: specialized knowledge, theoretical and practical; and commitment to standards of competence and excellence with the objective of serving others. One may argue that the theoretical component of knowledge is more distinctive in ministry than in other professions. While it is important for ministers to have command of practical techniques such as public speaking, teaching, and counseling, these techniques are not unique to ministry. It is theological understanding, the thinking through of the "content of faith," in Barth's phrase, that determines or should determine the ways in which techniques are to be used to serve in Christ's name. Theological competence, furthermore, is fundamental to the teaching function and to the "watching brief" that is a distinctive responsibility of the ordained minister within the whole ministry of the church. Theological capability is fundamental to the understanding and use of appropriate authority by ministers. Competence in the ministry is sustained by means of continuing study and reflection.

It is precisely here that a sense of professional responsibility, even a certain pride in being professional, is fitting. Unfortunately, there is disturbing evidence that Protestant clergy often do not succeed very well in sustaining high theological competency. Too many seem to follow no program of serious study at all after seminary. This may be caused by a feeling that theology is abstract and therefore irrelevant. That can happen to theology! To give reasons for questions about the actual life and work of a congregation that respond to theological criticism, to propose fresh directions, and to help members of a congregation understand is to be a teacher in the professional sense. Theology that has no relation to practice does not help in this task; but a practicalism divorced from theology may carry the church away from Christ.

There is an important difference between the ministry and other professions. In law and medicine, for example, the professionals are the only practitioners while the clients or patients are passive recipients, presumably the beneficiaries, of the expertise. This creates a great temptation for lawyers and doctors to become authoritarian in relating to clients and patients, a circumstance that is now being widely protested. The tendency in law and medicine toward independence of client or patient is intensified by the fact that these professionals are immediately responsible for their standards of practice not to those who seek their services but to a professional association of their peers, bar associations, or medical societies. Professional ministry, on the other hand, is part of a ministry of the whole church and in almost all churches, either by virtue of polity or custom, clergy are responsible to church bodies in which their "clients" have a voice.

## Church, Ministry, and Ministers

The difference between clergy and laity in the church helps us to understand the professional character of the ministry. A distinction that Hans Küng makes in his book *The Church* is helpful.[4] He distinguishes the "charismatic" from the "diaconal" ordering of the church. There are insights here concerning both ministry and other professions, particularly the differing relationships between professionals and their clients/patients on the one hand and, on the other, the clergy and parishioners.

As with Schillebeeckx, Küng sees the church as a charismatic community in which all share the new life in Christ generated by the Spirit. At this fundamental level there is no distinction between clergy and laity but simply a single ministry to which all are called. "Priesthood" is a priesthood of the church as such. "Clergy" comes from *kleros*, which means "share." All believers share in "eschatological salvation" that God gives to each member of the church.[5] St. Paul's view of the church is thoroughly charismatic and there is no permanent, institutionalized ordination to clerical ministry. There is a definite ordering of the church's life based upon differing particular gifts of the Spirit and these issue in a functional division of labor within the undivided ministry. The church is a "fellowship of the gifts of the Spirit."[6] Distinctions within the ministry, however, remained at first imprecise and fluid.

In time need arose for a more formal structuring of the church. Already in the pastoral epistles and the Acts we see evidence of a developing institutionalism. Eventually there arose both a distinction between clergy and laity and gradations within the clergy—bishop, priest or presbyter, deacon. This becomes the "diaconal" order. Küng, like Schillebeeckx, sees this development as having gone too far. Distinctions of function and authority begin to take priority over the more unified community with its broadly distributed spiritual gifts within a common ministry. Küng suggests that the view of priests as a separate class granted the exclusive power through ordination to convey sacramental grace to the people arose in post-New Testament times in conjunction with the idea of the mass as a "new sacrifice" which is made by the priest for the people, one performed in addition to the once-for-all sacrifice of Christ. Grace (*charisma*) came to be seen as flowing through the priests to the people rather than being granted to the community as a whole and only then administered in various ways through diaconal ordering. Organizational forms, in short, became disconnected from their charismatic base.

75

The institutional and charismatic orders should be "correlative," states Küng, with the charismatic order primary. Formal organizational structures should be "rooted in *charisma*" and are primarily "a particular side and aspect of the general and fundamental charismatic structure of the church."[7] Sacraments and preaching of the Word are means of grace given to the church as a whole. Special ministries are instituted by ordination and are based on particular gifts of the Spirit for preaching, teaching, and the pastoral task. These ordinations are not meant to create a special class of people with an exclusive channel of special grace. Such a concept posits clergy as mediators between God and people but the gospel plainly states that there is only one Mediator, Jesus Christ. Insofar as there exists a mediatorial function in the church it belongs to the whole church and mediates the gospel to the world.[8]

Küng uses the term "diaconal" advisedly. The choice of "service" is meant to tell us that while a distinction between clergy and laity is appropriate to church order, it does not justify autocratic or excessively bureaucratic structures or notions of clerical callings as superior, much less doctrines that interpose clerics between God and his people.

This theological analysis contains a forceful suggestion for law and medicine. It is possible that lawyers and doctors might see themselves as functioning within the context of fundamental communities, the one devoted to the cause of justice and the other to that of health. The relations between professionals and lay persons in these fields are now defined by institutional structures rather than overarching human communities. In the present institutional setting, differences between the experts and the clients or patients are dominant. The experts are "mediators" of special knowledge and technique and the clientele is passive recipient of expert ministrations. The tendency of the present system is to define professionals as members of a social elite with special privileges and prerogatives. Resentment against this apparent professional aristocracy seems to be fuelling reactions among lay persons as evidenced in assertions of patients' autonomy and rights, suspicions that professionals have allowed the motive of service to be eclipsed by love of wealth, criticism of the inclination of professionals to gather protectively around their own incompetents, malpractice suits, and resentment of the lobbying of professional associations against legislation threatening to their self-interest.

If there were a concept of communities that could parallel for law and medicine the charismatic concept of the church, professionals and lay persons could unite in commitment to certain values and goals.

These would define their common "faith" and activities aimed at realizing them would constitute their "ministry," the service of professionals. Since all of us are at least potential clients or patients, we could then approach problems in law and medicine united in a common effort to utilize resources to meet mutual needs. This would certainly result in giving laity a voice in some matters of professional practice and this is being done in some professional ethics committees. Nevertheless, the strangeness of these suggestions to other professions underscores the unique content of professional clergy practice.

None of this denies the importance of expertise. There are technical issues on which lay people are not competent to make judgments. Neither should we fail to honor the motives of service and moral dedication that exist among professionals. Clergy have their own temptations and failings, and are not more moral than persons in other professions. We simply mean that to think of one's profession as grounded in a larger community of common values and aims undergirds the motive of service and quells tendencies toward greed, pursuit of social status, and other motives that threaten true professionalism. It also reinforces the understanding that the professions exist to meet human needs in society and therefore, in a sense, belong to society itself. Professionals are stewards as well as practitioners.

Those who argue that there is a place for a society of peers in professional ministry, as Dr. James Glasse has contended,[9] merit respect but we believe that it is better to ground the profession in a community that unites professional clergy and lay believers on a basic level of equality and mutuality.

## Humility in Professionals

We have taken pains in this book to distinguish between an attitudinal humility that betrays lack of confidence and impairs competence in pastoral practice and what we here term "professional humility."

*While a graduate student at Harvard University, the writer of this paragraph took a guided reading course with a professor whose role, according to the catalogue, was to see the students periodically to discuss agreed-upon readings. Professor A., however, was so engrossed with extracurricular activities that he repeatedly cancelled appointments. In one semester, for example, there were only two meetings. Arriving at the point where a choice of advisors for the doctoral dissertation had to be made, the student searched the faculty*

*for the professor whose field best fitted his choice of subject. He
learned by chance that Professor A. fully expected to direct the
dissertation. The student asked whether Professor A. in fact had time
to do it. He refused the question and replied: "There is nobody else
in the faculty qualified to advise you." Whereupon this writer
modified the dissertation proposal and bade farewell to Professor A.*

Professional humility is capable of responding to the need for professional services, even when the student (or person served) is a bit
cheeky. Persons paying for services have a right to question professionals
within the limits of courtesy. Professional humility is a commitment to
respond in terms of service that meets need. It overrides pride, pique,
and much else.

Professional humility requires that a pastor or lay minister deal pa-
tiently and at reasonable length with those who are troubled by the
church professional's judgments and behavior. It is arrogance to dismiss
as obvious fools those who disagree or misunderstand. Even when they
annoy, the professional is committed to serve them and is not their
judge. The professional mind is always inquiring: "What is the appropriate response in these circumstances to help this person?" When a
qualified and conscientious professional has been affronted by an ignorant patient/client/counselee, it tests professional humility to choke
back a dismissive response and instead to ask oneself: "What do I do
now to help this person?" If termination of the relationship must occur,
it should not be the result of a surge of resentment but an answer to
the above question. If anything is to be accomplished for the person,
another professional may well have to be recommended.

It is an act of professional humility to refer a person to another
professional who is better qualified than oneself or to whom the individual can relate better than to oneself. Referral is so common among
physicians and lawyers as scarcely to appear in this light, but the same
is not true of those doing professional ministry. Nevertheless, the pastor
and lay associates in ministry are general practitioners of the ministry
and cannot be equally well informed in every area of religious leadership.
Ministers should experience no embarrassment in saying to a lay person
who has asked a particular question or expressed a special need: "Let
me help you get in touch with Ms. Jones. She knows more about that
problem than I do."

Ministers may also find occasion to refer dissatisfied parishioners to
another congregation where the ministry and fellowship are better suited

to them. It is not a referral, however, to communicate the message: "If you don't like it here, why don't you just buzz off?" however adroitly concealed the dismissive spirit may be.

The pastor who has learned to think ethically will have no difficulty in identifying many other occasions when professionally disciplined humility is demanded. More will be said of this in a later chapter.

## Word and Sacrament in Church and Ministry

In most denominations the preaching of the Word and the administration of the sacraments are reserved for the ordained ministry. We have also connected the teaching function of the clergy with its specifically professional character. Do these functions properly define and distinguish the clergy profession?

We believe that such a distinction is misleading. It tends to obscure the fact that Word and Sacrament belong to the whole church, so they cannot be the means for distinguishing the clergy office from the laity. The teaching (or theological) role alone may not be a fully sufficient criterion of the clerical ministry but at least it clearly distinguishes the professional office of minister from lay offices in the church. To deny Word and Sacrament to the church by concentrating them in the hands of the clergy is not only to professionalize Word and Sacrament but also falsifies the church by making the clergy its very custodians. The church as such is not so focused in the clergy alone as to justify the exclusive identification of Word and Sacrament with professional ministry. Word and Sacrament are *charisma*, gifts of the Spirit, to the whole body of believers. It is the church that is the residence of the Word of God and the sacraments by which believers live. The clergy are not their custodians on behalf of all. God gives gifts without clerical mediation or custody.

It is at the diaconal level of ordering that churches have decided to assign the preaching and teaching of the Word and the administration of the sacraments to the clergy.

To be sure, these roles require particular gifts of the Spirit and churches must take care to determine that candidates have both the talent and training to perform them effectively. But diaconal decisions do not remove the *charisma* from the church as a whole nor may they be regarded as unique to the clergy.

Hans Küng contends that whatever differentiations may be made in diaconal ordering, all church members should have some active part in preaching and clerical ministrations. He adds that while not all have the gifts to be regular preachers to the congregation, lay preaching should be allowable in the church's rules.[10] As for sacraments, the Roman Catholic church already allows lay members to administer baptism and absolution under special circumstances such as an emergency. Why not, asks Küng, allow the same for ordination and celebration of the Lord's Supper? Further, the main reason for this may not really be emergency. Can we afford to rule out the possibility of a recurrence of the situation in the Pauline churches where a ministry including sacraments was conducted in a "charismatic" situation? Can we exclude the possibility of an outpouring of the Spirit on a congregation that would then celebrate the sacraments without conforming to ordinary organizational rules and procedures?[11]

Most Protestant churches provide for lay preaching, although it is usually reserved for special occasions. It seems inconsistent that most of them do not affirm the same thing in regard to sacramental celebrations. Perhaps this is the continuing influence of Schillebeeckx's second concept of ministry by which ordination is thought to bestow a special power upon the cleric that alone can validate a sacrament. Even Protestant practice appears sometimes to assume that divine grace comes through clergy to people rather than being bestowed first upon the whole *laos* of God.

Hendrik Kraemer has spoken of an "unfinished reformation,"[12] arguing that both Luther and Calvin in their doctrines of vocation and the priesthood of all believers broke down the clericalist view of the church and ministry. In their treatments of the "marks" of the true church, however, they reverted to a clericalistic view, contends Kraemer. In addition to the traditional four marks (*notae*: unity, apostolicity, holiness, universality), they added two that were to prove decisive: true preaching of the Word and celebration of the sacrament "according to the institution of Christ" (in the Calvinist wording). In the sixteenth century these functions were assigned to clergy. The question is: Why should they remain exclusively clerical roles?

In sum, to define the professional ministry as distinctively a ministry of Word and Sacrament is to risk obscuring the fact that Word and sacraments belong primarily and essentially to the ministry of the church as a whole. The clergy–laity distinction is appropriate only at the diaconal level. Different forms of diaconal ministry are indeed based upon various "charismatic" gifts[13] and so may not be disconnected from the basic charismatic ministry. But diaconal ministries allow or demand additional specialization. Among these services the clergy require special theological and practical education. This leads us to the following conclusions:

—Word and Sacrament belong to the least specialized level of ministry. The Bible is to be read by all. Word and Sacrament represent what is essential to the gospel, to faith, to the whole ministry, and to every particular ministry. There is no ministry that is not a ministry of Word and Sacrament.

—Even at this basic and charismatic level particular gifts suggest a division of labor within ministry. But not exclusively! All members of the church bear responsibility for the whole ministry. Everyone should proclaim the Word; in other words, be evangelists and witnesses. Everyone should be a pastor to others as the priesthood of all believers implies. Everyone teaches others, as Christian parents are called to do with their children. At the same time, different gifts will be recognized. Some persons will make better preachers, teachers, pastors, "leaders," and "rulers" (to use Schillebeeckx's terms) than others.

—In the diaconal ordering of ministry, specialization properly occurs. Those called to clerical ministry are appropriately given special theological training. Why? Clergy have special responsibility for the watching brief over the ministry of the whole church. While they do not do all the teaching in the church, they carry responsibility to "teach the teachers." As a matter of appropriate diaconal ordering they are given regular but not exclusive responsibility for preaching and presiding over sacramental celebrations.

Preaching requires more specialized knowledge and technique than the administration of sacraments, yet lay preaching is widely permitted. Presiding over sacramental observances can be taught very readily. If ordination does not bestow special sacramental power denied to the church as a whole, there seems little reason to exclude lay persons from this role.

For these reasons we consider the professional clerical ministry to be distinguished by its responsibilities for theology and teaching. Clergy are professionals who are expected to be competent and to maintain standards of excellence in the performance of the duties that distinguish them from others in the church. The professional ethics of the clergy rest upon a clear discernment of its fundamental character, its duties, and standards. We shall now turn to an examination of cases that help to clarify the principles of an appropriately practiced authority and professionally competent teaching and other applications of theological understandings.

# 5

## Practicing the Pastor's Authority

The examples of clergy behavior cited in earlier chapters touch the problem of authority in ministry at a very tender spot: the intrusion of the purely human self of the minister upon clerical roles. The issues we will examine here focus closely on the person of the pastor and call for self-examination. It is futile to treat ethics as a matter of rules and guidelines essentially dissociated from the inner life of the professional person. Where there is no commitment of conscience to a truly diaconal life, rules of ethics can at best define and help to prevent the worst unprofessional behavior.

### Preaching as an Ego Trip

What are we to make of such feelings as that confessed by the pastor who admitted that when he preached the Word he sometimes felt almost like God? True, the Word has authority and should be preached with authority; but how do we sort out the authority of the Word from egoistic authority feelings? Sometimes we seem to speak with too little authority. One is reminded of the old-time preacher who excoriated a particular sin in his parish as "that foul belch from the bowels of hell!" Although it is gone from the modern pulpit, royal purple rhetoric in its own time did express authority. The fact that we are now more lavender than purple in our way of expressing ourselves is largely a matter of changed cultural styles. In the Victorian age more authority was granted to parents, teachers, bosses, officials, and professionals.

Yet we are not without our own subtle temptations. For instance, what of the ministers, who insistently put their church members right on a variety of theological and social issues? Their views follow a particular pattern of one sort or another, liberal or conservative, and their preaching rarely intimates that the issues allow for honest differences of opinion. Most pastors with some experience have outgrown such unself-conscious naivete, yet any time we plunge through the ifs, ands, and buts of issues in order to hit them head-on it is hard to be sure that we are proclaiming God's Word and not merely our own convictions.

One way of measuring our own ego involvement is to ask ourselves how well we respond to criticism. Some criticism is ill-informed, to be sure. Where we honestly think we are correct we should stick to our guns. Some criticism is merely ill-tempered. Other complaints touch our abilities and techniques: we may need, for example, some sharpening of public speaking skills. But almost all criticism hurts. How are we handling that? Do we hurt for the sake of the Word and the purity and integrity of its exposition or for our own egos, which are so exposed in our preaching? We must put ourselves on the line in public constantly and the more we put into sermon preparation and delivery the more vulnerable we are to being hurt.

In professional life there is an important role for lay criticism. Some denominational policies call for periodic review and evaluation of pastors' work by representatives of the congregation. These programs provide an occasion for self-examination with regard to ego-involvement in the several aspects of ministry. But professional pride can easily resent criticism from "mere" lay people, as some might put it. It may furnish some consolation to readers of this book to know that seminary professors are subject to student evaluation of their teaching. Just how qualified is a student to criticize a professor? you may ask. Such evaluation has a valid place in professional life, notwithstanding the fact that skeptical questions are raised in academia as elsewhere about the value of such procedures.

## Adulation and the Personality Cult

Pastors who have been raked by severe criticism find attitudes of adulation hard to comprehend. They would like to experience a little of it themselves! Paradoxically, adulation may be produced from the same root as exaggerated criticism: namely, the decline of all authority in modern social life. In most forms of Protestantism there is an individualism that maintains that every Christian is her or his own authority in religious matters and that there is no such thing as an expert in matters such as religion and politics. This rejection of authority is no doubt reinforced by the anti-intellectualism that persists in American culture.[1] Yet many church members long for leaders they can trust and the strong desire for authority within them takes the minister as its object. But ministers are no longer institutional authority figures with powers of enforcement, so the authority granted may be withdrawn as it was given: in consequence of a purely personal inclination. The disappointment of exaggerated expectations turns many ministers from saints they never were to demons they can never become.[2]

As a rule church people tend to deal gently with the clergy. They praise and support us when they can. It is considered good manners to greet the minister after the service with a kind word about the sermon. Barring behavior that gratuitously forfeits public respect, the minister enjoys a certain position in the community. This respect is not the same as that granted the movers and shakers of our society. Business moguls, scientists and political officials all outrank us in this regard. But many people distinguish between materialistic or power-oriented values and values that are moral and spiritual, and clergy are widely looked upon as experts in these latter values. Rightly or wrongly the clergy symbolize the spiritual realities to which many people are committed. In offering us their respect, many church members are expressing their faith in the gospel. This makes it all the more difficult for clergy to distinguish between respect for the faith and appreciation of themselves.

Some might suppose that the more diffident clergy would be less vulnerable to sins of pride. In reality the more self-confident may be better able to look at things objectively and take the measure of adulation realistically while those with less confidence may be more tempted to vanity by praise, even the most conventional. Ego temptations frequently result in specific ways of behaving or operating in ministry and such manifestations of egoism call for reflection and correction.

The cult of personality is a common phenomenon in American Protestant church life. The scenario goes something like this:

> Pastor S. is called to a local congregation that has problems but is basically sound and has potential. The previous pastorate has been a difficult one. Pastor S. is able; she has "charisma." A few members leave at the outset of her ministry but others are added to the

*membership. The congregation thrives. Budget and programs expand.
After ten years of steady progress Pastor S. leaves for another
charge. When new Pastor J. is called, something becomes evident
that was not evident earlier: An unexpectedly large number of
members leave; apparently they were attached to Pastor S.
personally, since their complaints boil down to the fact that Pastor J.
is not Pastor S.! Their fidelity, it turns out, was not so much to the
church and its beliefs as to Pastor S. and many ceased attending
worship altogether. Pastor S. may have done everything in her power
to impress on parishioners that loyalty to Christ and the church is
central, not loyalty to the pastor. Yet the phenomenon persists.*

One denomination conducted a study a few years ago in order to
understand how a few congregations managed to thrive during this time
of general decline in many churches. The answer in nearly every case
was that the pastor was the key. We may be thankful for effective
clerical ministries while still being uneasy about the excessive dependence of some congregations on one person. To do everything possible
to counteract this tendency is, if nothing else, crucial to a pastor's own
spiritual well-being.

### The Pastor as Dictator-Controller

The more successful the pastor the greater the temptation to run
things one's own way and the more one is admired, loved, even revered,
the easier it is to become a genial dictator. The tendency toward this
particular ego trip is reinforced by the fact that over a period of time
members are attracted by the personality of the pastor with a consequent
inclination in the congregation to endorse programs he or she has
introduced. Lay people who propose alternatives tend to be winnowed
out of the leadership, even the membership. Aggressively developing
societies do not argue with success. The authoritarian minister fits the
model of business that allows a strong and able person to run the show.
There is nothing wrong with efficiency in business or church life and
useful models for ministry can be found in many fields but they are
often misapplied.

There is a particular psychological factor that is often related to
authoritarian behavior among clergy: namely, the need to control.

*Pastor H. was a remarkable person. Becoming pastor of a tiny
congregation shortly after the First World War, he worked steadily as*

*his community grew until at his retirement the congregation had grown from 300 to 2000 members and under his successors the momentum continued. This was an entirely independent congregation with neither conference, presbytery, or diocese to assist financially or in resolving problems, yet never from the time Pastor H. assumed the pastoral responsibility did it experience any serious division. This was not because there were no stresses; there were the usual staff problems and divisive issues. The secret of Pastor H.'s success lay in his extraordinary pastoral devotion coupled with a tight control of every aspect of church life and program. He selected the governing boards personally which, while elected by the congregation, were composed of members who knew his wishes, respected his success, and loved him for being with them in their times of pain. Pastor H. wanted nothing but the prosperity of his church. He never troubled himself about money, pension, or any other financial considerations and his family saw little of him. He ruled his household strictly and no one in or out of the family doubted his priorities. The church came first.*

Pastor H. was selfless in every regard but one: it was absolutely crucial to him to maintain control of every program, including his family (which sometimes felt like one of his "programs"!). While his pastoral effectiveness stood on its own feet it was also powerful politics. Who could cross a man who had given himself so completely to others? It was a sacrilege to stand apart from such dedication and formulate judgments on his work. The few who could escape the power of his personality recognized in Pastor H. a man to whom it was important psychologically to maintain control of his environment. No one understood this better than his grown children. Pastor H. did not come across as a dictator because he was never in a hurry and he never silenced a discussion. He just waited and in the end, everything went his way. He lost battles but he always won the war.

It could hardly be said that this pastor was unethical. One of his strengths was his utter integrity. Yet the fact remained that his will prevailed absolutely in the church and persons who found this uncongenial quietly went elsewhere. No one would have been more surprised than he at the analysis presented here. He could conceive no other way of conducting the affairs of a congregation than his own.

More obvious ethical questions can be raised about some of the techniques used by pastors who cannot dominate through service as Pastor H. did. Pastors and professionals in ministry almost inevitably, for example, acquire a circle of member-friends who are particularly supportive. This is simply a fact of parish life. Church professionals may use these folk as an informal cabinet of advisors and supporters, forming a kind of cabal that decides agendas and takes political steps to assure acceptance of the pastor's views. A certain amount of politicking is endemic to any organization. It goes wrong when some church members are denied a voice.

The diaconal ordering of a church, including its polity, has both theological and ethical purpose. Presbyterians are fond of saying that things should be done "decently and in order." They are not alone in this: the procedures by which a church is governed should manifest an understanding of justice grounded in the reality of Christian community. A church is a covenanted community. Its members are essentially equal ("neither Jew nor Greek, slave nor free, male nor female" [Gal. 3:28]), a priesthood that embraces all believers. This commitment calls for openness and mutuality, whatever the polity. Whether the polity is hierarchical, representative, or democratic, members have a right to expect that the agreed order will be respected. "Railroading" by definition is a violation of order and cannot be defended by either justice or love.

### The Pastor as *Factotum*

The pastor who does it all is a phenomenon often associated with authoritarianism but there are overbusy pastors who would be surprised and hurt at such a suggestion. Pastors may estimate themselves modestly but still gather too much of the ministry of the congregation into their own hands. Hyperconscientiousness sometimes accounts for this mistake. Even pastors aware of such a tendency in themselves may be unable to avoid the problem in a small congregation. Lack of lay leadership may be actually the fact but sometimes it covers an unwillingness to delegate. Where pastors are at fault, the cause may be a working assumption that the ministry belongs primarily to them. The temptation is subtle because it travels in the sheep's clothing of conscientiousness and willingness to work twelve hours a day, seven days a week for the gospel's sake.

### The Pastor as Manipulator

False exercise of authority more readily occurs through manipulation than through bald domination.[3] Consciously or unconsciously, pastors find ways to keep people dependent on them. There are myriad ways to do this.

> *"You know," said a man to his wife as they left the worship service, "I'm getting pretty tired of this guilt trip the preacher keeps laying on us." "Oh, Charles," she replied, "you're too critical. Besides, what he says is true! We are all sinners and the things he points to are real enough." "I grant that," said Charles. "It's the way he does it. I get the feeling that he is laying it on us to keep us convinced that we have a problem to which he has the answer. That keeps us feeling dependent on the church and gives him a pretty important role too. Sometimes I think that with the clergy having less prestige and influence than they'd like, ministers grab at whatever gives them some sense of power. Then they beat us over the head with it." "I still think you're being unfair to him." "Mildred, you're too kind! It's part of what I love about you but you lean so far over backward to be fair that someday you're going to fall and fracture your skull."*

The capacity to feel guilt is essential to normal personality and the appeal to guilt is a proper part of the gospel proclamation. Yet a great deal of manipulation by clergy involves improper appeals to guilt or even the deliberate exciting of guilt feelings.

Let us be clear about true guilt and the minister's proper relation to it. The news is good because it is the news that our inveterate sinfulness has been decisively dealt with! "The good that we would, we do not; the evil that we would not, that we do" (Rom. 7:19; author's paraphrase). Christians believe that none of us can rescue ourselves from the vicious circle of pride and sin. The notion of sin does not mean that there is no good at all in us. It is rather that all that is good and right in us is skewed. Doing evil is like coasting downhill whereas doing right is an uphill struggle. Persons who are convinced of this—and we do our best to persuade them—are bound to carry some burden of guilt. Who knows what regrets are hidden in the hearts of parishioners? Precisely at this point the proclaimer of the Word comes to the rescue. There is forgiveness for all our sins. Mercy and reconciliation, justification and peace of heart and mind await us. All that is needed is faithful acceptance of the message. But who bears the message? The pastor! So the pastor seems to be the conduit of redeeming grace. The pastor is needed.

To those traditions that do not stress original sin as much as Lutherans and Presbyterians, for example, this statement of the case for guilt may seem overblown. But all Christians recognize the themes of guilt and forgiveness in the gospel and, Christian dogmas apart, people do have guilt feelings. The question for pastors is how we can address these realities and proclaim the answer offered in the gospel without intruding ourselves as mediators, as indispensible grace-dispensing functionaries, and so implying to people like Charles that ordinary mortals must look to us for forgiveness.

We may think that such notions of original sin and persistent guilt are passé in the modern world and in some quarters no doubt they are. William Temple once remarked that when you accuse many moderns of being miserable sinners they will deny it because they are perfectly happy sinners—at least for a while. Yet modern psychotherapy has shown that guilt feelings may become excessive, paralyzing, and very damaging.

People have guilt feelings that make them vulnerable to manipulation and dependence. Sometimes pastors develop a "gut instinct" for the exploitation of guilt, a talent that we may not understand objectively. Manipulators? Never! But what would a psychiatric analysis of our sermons over a period of time reveal? Have we prayerfully and earnestly examined our inner motives as we choose what we will say, and how? How about our financial appeals? Is there ever an undertone in our promotion that suggests that giving can exorcise guilt?

All manipulation is wrong because it uses and demeans persons. The most radical doctrine of sin should never obscure the basic Christian affirmation of the intrinsic worth of persons and of God's purpose to restore them to the "glorious liberty of the children of God" (Rom. 8:21), not to dependence on the clergy. The redemptive process is hindered when the manipulative pastor intrudes.

Psychologists tell us that some people nevertheless seek an authority figure. They really want a relationship of dependency. Far from taking personal advantage of this, pastors need to be competent to help their parishioners attain "the stature of the fulness of Christ" (Eph. 4:13). In St. Paul's theology Christian maturity is not an isolated individualism but responsible membership in a community of love and mutuality. This is neither dependence nor independence but interdependence. Human beings "in Christ" are not to be less human but more so. We are dependent on God, interdependent with one another. These should not be confused with a crippling dependency on other human beings, including those called to proclaim God's Word.

Possibilities for the imposition of pastors' egos on people abound when a congregation gathers for worship on Sunday morning. In a sense, this is a captive audience. Military chaplains in World War II were sometimes embarrassed by overly cooperative commanding officers who marched members of their commands to worship services, but no one is forced into local churches. Many attend simply because their faith impels them. Yet faith creates obligation. Parishioners have needs that they recognize and they believe that religion is important and that they should attend church.

There is a special aura about Sunday worship. Some attend no other church activities. A few may have a half-superstitious feeling about this central church function. For many reasons, a deeply rooted sense of obligation toward worship is widespread.

The worship service is housed beautifully and carefully planned and the minister is the principal actor. It is a natural setting for a cult of personality. No one answers back. When the moment for preaching comes the lights go down everywhere except the pulpit, a hush falls over the audience, and all eyes focus (at least until someone's eyelids droop) on the robed figure bathed in a nimbus of holy light. What an invitation to an ego trip, first class! We would not be surprised to see angels ascending and descending along the lighted pathway to heaven. The Word is about to be spoken! Who would not occasionally be tempted to take personal advantage of this sort of situation?

To subject worshipers to sermons lacking adequate exegetical or theological foundations and devoid of insightful life applications is an imposition and betrays an ego that believes so serenely in its own merit that no real service (in this case, the announcement of the gospel and teaching) can be rendered. Pastors do not all have to be, nor can many become great preachers. But they must all prepare their sermons. Many gifts are ideally desirable in clerical ministry and almost no one has them all. It is also true that pressures on pastors can intrude on time that belongs to sermon preparation. In a busy week, something may be slighted. Most church members understand these things and are surprisingly forgiving, even indulgent. They like their minister—and he or she may be tempted to trade on that. If members consider their pastors especially able in other phases of ministry, they will genuinely love and respect them for that and will keep coming to church. But they are not fooled. As a friend of this writer said of her pastor and close friend: "Well, you know, L. does pretty much as he pleases!" A member who is as loyal as she is sophisticated is entitled to sermons that are carefully prepared.

A preacher has the difficult task of trying to distinguish between a faithful proclamation of Christian truth and earnestly believed personal or party ideas. No handy rule of thumb resolves the problem. An honest pastor may provide occasions when parishioners can challenge what has been said in sermons. The process is encouraged when judgments are offered in a tentative spirit as St. Paul did on at least one occasion. "Now concerning the unmarried I have no command of the Lord but I give my opinion as one who by the Lord's mercy is trustworthy" (1 Cor. 7:25). Sometimes we must speak without claiming divine authority.

The ethical bind of the preacher is relieved somewhat as lay people increasingly think theologically. There should be a close connection between preaching and adult education. In the perspective of Hebrews 5 growth in understanding the content and implications of faith is part of growth in grace and the Christian life. From Ephesians 4 we gather that such growth is to occur in community and mutuality: "And his gifts were that some should be apostles, some prophets, some evangelists, some pastors and teachers, to equip the saints, for the work of ministry, for building up the body of Christ, until we all attain to the unity of the faith and of the knowledge of the Son of God, to mature manhood, to the measure of the stature of the fulness of Christ" (Eph. 4:11-13).

Part of our ministry is to foster growth into a more profound unity of congregational faith and life, especially in the struggle to understand the implications of our faith for being Christian in the contemporary world. The sermon alone is a one-way communication and may end by being used manipulatively; but it can be a useful voice in a dialogue of growth when coupled with programs where "come-back" is invited. This sort of active lay involvement functions as a useful counterweight to the ego temptations of the clerical ministry.

As a check to ego temptation, it is valuable to remember that lay members are meant to be active participants in what the clergy and church staff do. The pastoral prayer, for example, is the prayer of the whole people voiced by the worship leader. The pastor or lay minister has the responsibility to help the congregation understand that it is not an audience that has come to be entertained by a performance but a community of believers gathered to hear and meditate upon the Word together. Hearing, like speaking, can be responsible or irresponsible.

A common abuse of pastoral authority lies in the posing of artificial problems to which the minister as preacher then offers a particular version of the gospel as the only answer. Reinhold Niebuhr once observed that the trouble with much preaching is that the preacher spends too much time answering questions that nobody has asked. Niebuhr was an effective apostle to unbelievers and was very sensitive to the wide discrepancy between the discourse within the walls of the church and the church's need to be heard on the streets. A minister may preach very acceptable sermons, yet rarely touch the actual problems of the members of that parish, not to speak of those who are discouraged with religion. The special state of mind that prevails at Sunday worship, the "holy situation," may produce an unreal atmosphere. Under its spell unreal questions may for the moment take on plausibility, favored by a temporary suspension of the congregation's critical faculties. Round phrases punctuated by authoritative gestures may briefly hypnotize the listeners until they come to their senses and realize that the preacher did not say very much after all.

## The Watching Brief

The watching brief of the professional clergy defends not only the integrity of the gospel and the pastoral calling but also stands guard over the integrity of ministers themselves. If the clergy are to take responsibility for the integrity of the teaching activity in the church, they must all the more conscientiously accept responsibility to watch over themselves. Pastors are professionals. They do not report to a supervisor. Pastors are answerable diffusely to the church at large, congregations and their officers, church judicatories, and ordinaries. In practice, professionals are almost entirely their own bosses.

The failure of the personal watching brief makes a pretense of all professions of calling to the ministry. Arrogance in any form paralyzes the conscientiousness without which professionals become insensitive to the need for the highest standards of performance and for responsiveness to criticism. To assume that because one is a theological graduate, ordained and legitimately placed in a pastorate, one is therefore fitted for the ministry, is perhaps the most widespread misunderstanding of the authority of the clergy.

Nothing can defeat professional arrogance except a humility that is always ready and able to listen and that constantly prays, with the Psalmist: "Behold, thou desirest truth in the inward being; therefore teach me wisdom in my secret heart. . . . Create in me a clean heart, O God, and put a new and right spirit within me" (Ps. 51:6, 10). Such a plea is the prayer of those who profess above all to be faithful disciples of Jesus Christ. For the pastor in particular, God's gifts of grace in response to such a prayer are the very substance of the ministry.

# PART THREE

# CHARACTER & RELATIONSHIPS

# 6

## The Pastor as Human Being

Persons called to the clergy profession live always in the tension between two realities: their humanity—who and what they are, their best and their worst, their gifts and their limits—and the special demands of their calling. Three kinds of problems are generated by this tension.

The first is posed by the fact that theological definitions of ministry tend to be idealized descriptions of what ministry should be at its best, a standard that few if any can achieve. While this is partly because of the nature of theological definitions, it also reflects the unique character and special intensity of the call to ministry. This standard is a necessary challenge to better performance but it can also be deeply troubling when pastors are acutely aware of their human limitations. Many wonder whether they are up to the job or have mistaken their calling. Adding to the pressure is the widespread expectation that clergy should be special embodiments of the faith and morality they teach and preach.

The second problem is the clash between job demands and personal commitments to family, financial concerns, and health and recreation. Here the professional conscience deals with allocation of time and energy. Closely tied to this is the third problem, which is more subtle: the tension between the human individuality of ministers, lay or ordained, and the professional mold into which they are expected to fit. Has a minister a right to a particular life-style? Is self-fulfillment a legitimate ethical concern? May it be overridden by the demands of calling?

### Perfectionism and the Minister

Because of their humanity ministers are never quite up to the job. Some of them commit gross and obvious moral offenses. We have said from the beginning that such offenses lie outside the subject matter of this book. But about the more egregious offenses we make two observations. First, when such incidents occur, church authorities usually recognize that Christians are to season judgment with mercy. Justice must be served but so must forgiveness and reconciliation. Depending on their response, erring humans, including clergy, should be given another chance. Where that fresh beginning is denied it must be evident that basic qualifications such as honesty and commitment to the gospel of Christ are lacking.

Second, we regret that the offenses about which churches become most upset are so often limited to sex and money—for example, pastors who do not pay their bills or who misappropriate church funds. These are serious offenses—but are they really less tolerable in a professional church leader than racist or sexist attitudes or unconcern for the sufferings of the poor and oppressed? The scandal of the Bakkers and the PTL ministry that broke in 1987 involved sexual misbehavior, misuse of funds, and charges of drug addiction. A number of commentators expressed the view that their most serious offense, however, was their exploitation of honest religious sentiments for personal gain.

Ethical offenses, whether personal, social, or professional, radically contradict the expectations that people have of the clergy. These expectations reach into the minister's personal life. Are not pastors often faulted because they take a glass of wine, their children are obstreporous, or a profane word escapes their lips in a moment of exasperation? Some lay people have no problem with these very human traits, yet demand great sensitivity in their church professionals to issues such as peacemaking, economic justice, and racial and sexual equality. Expectations vary according to different understandings of faith, ethics, and ministry—and it adds up easily to a demand for perfection.

While parishioners can sometimes be hypercritical and overdemanding, they can also be remarkably gracious and forgiving. The minister's own conscience may well be the severest taskmaster. Hyperconscientiousness can lead to overwork, neglect of other responsibilities and, in extreme cases, to psychological breakdown and withdrawal from ministry.

Complicating all this is the fact that ministers can suffer from common psychological problems such as anxiety, anger, doubt, identity crisis, and a sense of powerlessness. Neither faith nor calling grants immunity from "the thousand shocks that flesh is heir to." For the pastor it is doubly painful to wonder why the message preached cannot be the cure of his or her own soul. Is the word we profess after all ineffective and our ministry a sham? There is great agony in the question of whether we have not ultimately betrayed the people we profess to love and serve.

Relief from the burdens of perfectionism in its many forms is not easy even though the answer is clear in Scripture. To appropriate the good news of grace and forgiveness is actually a daily necessity of the Christian life, not an emergency measure for crises only. We respect those who hold the doctrine of Christian perfection but we have never personally met a pastor or church professional who claimed to be perfect. They stumble and grope, fall and get up and fall again, along with their people. There is no cheap grace. Forgiveness and renewal come to those who are committed, who are fully aware that they have not attained the fullness of Christ. We do our work in the tension between moral and professional perfection and our painful incompleteness.

Conflict is often generated between minister and people when there are disparate understandings of faith and ministry. These differences need to be addressed as part of the teaching responsibility. They sometimes prove intractable but where there is genuine caring, biblical and theological interpretation of ministry is the ready instrument of reconciliation.

## Who Am I, Really?

One special tension is unique to professional life: Professions shape personhood. Individuals are marked in certain ways by their callings. A lawyer tends to think like a lawyer off the job. Pastors too can be expected to act consistently with their calling. A problem arises when a pastor may wonder: "Do I always have to conform? Why must I agree to be typed? What about my need to be myself, to have my own style?" We need to understand whether these are merely egoistic concerns or whether there are rights, even obligations, involved. Where is the line to be drawn between a properly humble submission on the one hand and mindless conformity on the other?

This has been called the issue of "role morality." Roles are ways in which we function in social and interpersonal relationships. Each of us plays many parts: husband or wife, friend, neighbor, citizen. Some roles are defined by occupation and all have ethical implications. Professionals have both the responsibility and the authority to do things that for others would be inappropriate or downright immoral. Cutting up another person's body is neither ethical nor legal for most of us, but surgeons are authorized to do it in the context of medical treatment—and no other!

Sometimes even sharper conflicts arise between role morality and personal morality. Lawyers among others face such problems. David Luban in *The Good Lawyer* focuses upon certain courtroom tactics that are approved, even required within the adversary system but that are at odds with the lawyer's personal moral standards.

> They must make truthful opposing witnesses look like liars or fools if they can; they must fight for their clients' "right" to oppress and exploit if the client wishes it; they must defeat just claims on technicalities if it can be done; they must keep information confidential though it means ruination for a hapless third party.[1]

Some lawyers defend such behavior by arguing that in their professional practice they are playing roles much like actors in the theater; professional behavior can be detached from real life morality. This argument is challenged by several contributors to Luban's volume. He notes that "lawyers—litigators in particular—often experience 'burnout' brought on by the moral tensions in their role."[2] Gerald Postema maintains that the attempt to live such a double life can only be achieved in the end by becoming the empty shell of a self. He points to Hannah Arendt's characterization of Rudolf Eichmann, who carried out the incredibly cruel and inhuman orders he was given by his Nazi commanders without any sense that there was something problematic about them. He had lost all psychological and moral self-definition and become a moral zombie.[3]

While pastors rarely encounter such obvious conflicts between professional and general morality, a problem remains: The roles demanded by the profession apply to all professionals whereas our humanity involves individuality and a sense of personal integrity.

We have argued in this book that truthfulness is fundamental to ethics. To be true to oneself is not only a matter of personal desire but also a moral imperative. An authentic individual is not an empty shell of customs, conventions, and cliches. The issue may be illustrated by considering two clergy types, deliberately caricatured.

Clergy A is a character straight out of television. He is a black-garbed figure of oppressive piety, furnished with a vocabulary of hackneyed religious phrases suited to every occasion. He is given to self-righteous moral judgments and lacks any understanding of the human situation. His personhood, if any is left, is awash in banality.

Pastor B, by contrast, is a free-wheeling, avant-garde, "with-it" person who defies most of the conventions and morality of the congregation and demands the right to be herself, to display an individual life-style. Her sense of self seems to overwhelm any regard for role requirements.

These extreme examples are rarely encountered but they dramatize a tension felt by many ministers. For every professional, the demands of both individual integrity and professional roles must be reconciled. It is not always clear exactly how they should be brought into balance. It may be just as important to respect the tension between them as to bring them into harmony.

Karen Lebacqz has made some very helpful observations about this tension.[4] She states that professional roles involve specifically professional obligations. Roles have to do with particular kinds of actions. Lebacqz is well aware that ethics has also to do with character. Character consists of those personality traits that are moral and have traditionally been called virtues. Actions both reveal our moral make-up and help to determine what we will become. When we go to a doctor or a lawyer, Lebacqz maintains, we are concerned not only about his or her technical competence, but even more about what *quality* of person he or she is. Being highly vulnerable, we want someone who is trustworthy, lest when we are in trouble, we become hurt even more. Can we entrust our well-being, perhaps our lives to these professionals? Professional ethics has a great deal to do with what sort of person the professional is.

Nevertheless, Lebacqz observes, it is dangerous to merge the self completely with professional roles.

> Carried to an extreme, people lose their personal identities and become totally identified with their roles, either by themselves or by others. We all know teachers who never stop being "teacher"—even when on a hike or at a birthday party. Ministers are often expected to be always in a ministerial role, available to listen and counsel and provide comfort. The women's movement has surfaced the anger many women feel when they are totally identified with a role such as wife or mother to the exclusion of their personal identity.
>
> Such a total identification with roles can be dangerous when it comes to ethics. The person may lose his or her ability to question the normal expectations that go with the role. We have come to expect politicians to lie but that does not make it right! . . . Indeed, we get our caricatures of professional groups—the stealthy lawyer, the overly pious minister—from taking to extremes the normal role morality of those groups.[5]

Totally to subordinate person to profession reduces the self to a caricature as we saw in the example of Clergy A above. On the other hand, for the minister of the Word, it is wrong to deny the subjection of self in fundamental ways to the demands of the calling (as distinct from "job" narrowly considered). Psychological health requires that life be integrated. Theologically speaking, those who cannot tolerate the demands of the calling must reconsider the genuineness of their call. There is no reproach in this. We make mistakes in religious matters as in all others.

The healthy self is the basis for critical response to role definitions and expectations, some of which are bound to be insupportable. In the language of H. Richard Niebuhr, the "responsible self" is basic to morality. In more specifically Christian terms, it is a self informed by grace. The effect of grace is to restore and support a true self in community with God and other human beings. Calling does not require us to cut the self to the pattern of social conventions, secular or religious.

Paul Tillich maintained that our lives are characterized by certain "polarities," tensions that relate like the positive and negative poles of a magnetic field.[6] If the two fall completely apart, something goes wrong. If one is dominated or absorbed by the other, things fall out of balance. To maintain that tension in ministry may be difficult but it is a source of creativity.

Our suggestion is that in ministry, role demands and the authentic self continually create tension. The problem is to turn tension to a creative purpose instead of being dismembered by it. In creative tension, each "pole" forms and shapes the other from within while maintaining a distance from the other. Without distance, neither can restrain the other's inherent excesses. Role demands are legitimate and need to be acknowledged; the same is true of the self.

If there is to be creative interaction between the self and its roles, we need to enlarge our view of the self. So far we have been considering the moral dimensions of the self and of professional roles. But when some ministers claim the right to their own life-styles they mean to include more than morality: for example, an idiosyncratic theology. A church professional who leans toward Pastor B is likely not only to be informal in dress and manner but also to be more individualistic in theology and choices of social involvement. Or such a person may opt for a nonsocial spiritualism. Specific personality formations go beyond minor differences of taste to different modes of thought and patterns of behavior. Along with these go differences in natural abilities. How are such facts to be weighed in pastors' decisions about the kinds of ministry they will choose and about where, when, and how they will perform them?

These issues will be discussed at greater length in chapter 8. Here we offer a few preliminary observations. It is inevitable and to some degree justified that personal characteristics should affect choices of ministry. Particular calls are certainly influenced by a pastor's style. The Protestant tendency toward personality cult in congregational life must be dealt with, not merely deplored. There are calls that will never be offered to a minister like Pastor B (or, oppositely, to Clergy A). Still, ministers need to ask themselves questions. Does my individual style come first or am I willing to modify it if effectiveness in ministry requires it? Is my ministry lopsided? Are there dimensions I am neglecting? How can I become more nearly "all things to all persons"? As I consider my talents, what should I make of biblical accounts of prophets and patriarchs whose calls have overridden their own sense of personal inadequacy?

These questions are raised as reminders that ministry cannot simply be accommodated to individual inclinations and preferences. Calling makes legitimate demands for change. We must make allowance for the Spirit of God who works when and where God chooses and has worked wonders despite the limits of an individual minister's abilities.

To have maturity of judgment means to understand the art of striking a happy balance between individual traits and role demands. No doubt this is more art than analysis, more prayer than thought, but thinking helps to define the right questions. We are thrust back upon what H. Richard Niebuhr, following Jonathan Edwards, called a judgment of the "fitting." There is no more exact standard for deciding aright.

## The Job and Its Limits

One aspect of maintaining the tension between the claims of self and role is the need for church professionals to protect certain parts of their lives from undue encroachment by the job. We do not entirely agree with James Glasse's proposal to regard ordained ministry basically as a job but it is helpful to understand that ministry is a job as well as a calling.

For many of us, a sense of calling is all it takes to make a job all-consuming. This tendency exists in all the traditional professions and is traceable in part to the time in western history when their practitioners were mostly clergy or monastics. In published standards of professional ethics, the professions still stress service as their primary motivation.

Professionals do not punch time clocks and their personal lives are more affected by work than in most other jobs. Like Caesar's wife, they are expected to be above reproach. All this is at least as true of clergy and professionals in ministry as of any others. To recognize that ministry is a job as well as a calling enables us to deal with our human limitations.

In emphasizing the high demands of calling, we must not confuse the sometimes exploitative behavior of church members with God's own summons to the ministry. Ministers may feel pressured to bow to the wishes of people who press personal agendas on them. But intrinsic to being a professional is the conviction that no one knows better than that professional how his or her work should be done. This means determining the allocation of time between work and recreation as well as between the many varieties of job responsibility. To be sure, pastors or lay ministers do not function in a vacuum, as though there existed no other centers of opinion or responsibility than their own: there are senior church authorities, congregational committees, and trusted advisors. Yet in planning and performing the whole range of parish work, the minister is not subject to direct supervision but is relatively autonomous. This freedom must be protected lest the quality of work be injured.

A "job"—the flow of work demanded from week to week—is not identical with a calling. God does not call God's servants to a life perpetually disturbed by church members skilled in arousing guilt feelings. Certain aspects of any job may provoke resentment year by year until a pastor greets retirement as a release from provocations. "Jobs" usually contain forces alien to calling and the mature professional knows what they are and deals with them summarily.

It is impossible to catalogue every job-related irritant that may threaten both personhood and professional effectiveness. These may include poor organization of one's work and/or personal time, difficulty in identifying persons to whom tasks may be delegated, growth in program and/or membership that becomes insupportable without additional staff, manipulative personalities, pressures that force ministers to work beyond their capacities, thus creating stress and interfering with health, financial anxieties, and myriad other troubles. All these are added to the normal stresses of private life. When this wretched list of demands is allowed to become overwhelming, professionals may leave jobs to which they still believe themselves called, or simply die.

What are the ethical issues here?

Job and calling may come into conflict in any position. Either may change. A job may cease to fit a calling, as often because one outgrows the job as because of "failure" in the job. So a first question is whether there is a sufficient correspondence between job and calling to make the fulfillment of calling possible. Candidness at this point saves a flood of stress and lays the basis for an ethically sound decision about continuence or termination. As a last resort one can protect oneself from a job by leaving it—not in trauma but in fulfillment of calling.

Ordinary job stresses can be dealt with by a series of protective measures. The church professional needs regular schedules of work, rest, exercise, and disciplined eating. A mix of public activity with private work—study, planning, prayer—that is suited to one's personality will help prevent burn-out.

Ministers feel constrained to be accessible. This is not the same as twenty-four-hour availability. Accessibility to parishioners is not a matter of submitting to whimsical interruption but of one's openness to them and willingness to take the time to meet their needs. That time can be planned—granted the inevitability of emergencies at inconvenient times!

*Pastor L. accepted a call to a congregation in Florida that had grown swiftly to 700 members but meanwhile had mishandled a building debt. The size of the congregation made the debt feasible but there was an enormous amount of work. Pastor L. wanted to be accessible and carried a beeper. Once the congregation became accustomed to his total availability, Pastor L. was ceaselessly interrupted in a job that particularly required control of his time. Unable to understand why he felt harassed, Pastor L. began to react to pressures erratically. He isolated himself from colleagues who could have advised him and, in the end, left not only the job but the ordained ministry.*

Failure to protect himself was substantially responsible for this pastor's flight. Getting a beeper expressed an idealism that was more than he— or perhaps any other pastor—could sustain. Pastor L.'s fundamental ethical failure was that he took too little account of himself—his own capabilities and physical and nervous strength—and thus failed on the job. Axiomatic to all ethical conduct is a realistic self-understanding.

Protecting oneself against the job is not a matter of accepting certain necessary but undesirable constraints. To build one's professional practice on the realities of the human self and to contain job demands within the limits which that self can fulfill responsibly is the truly ethical condition.

### The Two-Clergy Family

With the rapid increase in the number of ordained women in the Protestant churches there has arisen a new phenomenon: marriage between two ordained ministers and the development of two clergy careers in the same household. Special questions arise that call for carefully tailored solutions.

The churches that ordain women have concluded that there is neither theological nor ethical objection to the two-clergy household. The practical problems are gradually emerging and being worked out; as yet there can be no experts in this field of concern. The ethical questions that may exist must be separated out case by case.

*Bill and Wendy are both ordained Presbyterian ministers serving by joint appointment a parish in rural New York. They have six children so it is clear that there are at least two "jobs." They accepted the congregation's decision to pay one full-time salary, it being understood that Bill and Wendy would conduct the equivalent of one full-time ministry. They enjoy broad discretion in allocating the work of the church between them. Both Bill and Wendy and the congregation are well satisfied with the ministry thus arranged.*

Although it would be better if each spouse could receive a full salary, this plan meets a number of ethical concerns with imagination. The children see a great deal of both parents; Wendy preaches and administers the sacrament regularly and is not relegated to traditional women's areas of Christian education and parish visitation; Bill has no problem with his share of household tasks as well as child care. The tendency toward conflict between work and family that is so widespread among men who are both pastors and fathers is resolved by this shared ministry. The risk in this plan of joint minstry is that Bill and Wendy may steadily increase their workload until both in reality are underpaid.

Other clergy couples find arrangements more difficult.

*Walt and Betty married in early middle life, both having been divorced after considerable personal pain. It seemed best to relocate so they agreed that they would move to the area in which the first to receive a call found work and the other would seek a call within that area. Betty had recognized executive talents and was called to an administrative position in a church judicatory. Walt's search for work was difficult partly because his opportunities were limited by geography but more painfully because of a depression of spirit going*

*back to his divorce experience. They received counseling together
during this ordeal and when he finally was called as a parish minister
they felt themselves greatly blessed.*

In this example both Walt and Betty dealt openly with the complexities
of their two callings and shared the solution to the problems. There
were no problems of mutual jealousy and Walt did not feel put down
by Betty's early success in her job search. Strains on marriage can arise
around career rivalries between highly motivated professional couples,
however, and considerable ethical and psychological sensitivity is required of both partners.

The solutions to many of the problems now surfacing for clergy couples
lie with the churches themselves. Clergy and lay leaders have responsibility here—to acquaint churches of appropriate size and character
with the advantages of appointing a clergy couple, for example. In a
time of change the ethic of responsibility calls for creativity. Put oppositely, to be a faithful observer of the existing rules may not be enough
to meet ethical responsibility for the development of the church in new
ways.

## The Single Pastor

In Protestant churches there is a long-standing bias against the appointment of unmarried clergy. This goes back, at least in part, to the
reaction against clerical celibacy at the time of the Reformation and
is no doubt fed by the feeling that the married pastor is likely to be
more stable personally while the congregation runs fewer risks of embarrassment. Many find it hard to articulate the fear that the unmarried
may be homosexual, which works prejudicially to all the unmarried,
particularly the chaste among them, whatever their sexual inclinations.
Many people believe their congregations are better served by a couple,
perhaps an implicit confession that uncompensated service is expected
from the unordained spouse. Some remember the complications that
may ensue when a single male pastor courts and marries a young woman
in the congregation.

The changing marital situation of many pastors and candidates for
the ministry has increased the number of unmarried people seeking
pastoral calls, and the right of the single person to equal opportunity
is being ever more widely recognized today.

From an ethical perspective, there is no ground for discriminating
against the unmarried solely because they are single. Practical objections

to their appointment should be closely scrutinized for elements of prejudice. The single life is not morally inferior to married life and may, when undertaken sacrificially, be morally superior. Neither Jesus nor St. Paul chose to marry and their choices are understood and honored by the church if not much imitated. While Protestants reject any requirement of celibacy for clergy, we need to respect decisions not to marry, especially when vocationally motivated. To esteem those who have undertaken service that is not reconcilable with family responsibilities is an example of the balance between polarities that marks mature professional thinking.

## Considering New Calls

How is a pastor to decide when to take the initiative in making a change of position? What considerations come into play when an inquiry comes?

The question of when it is right and responsible to move from one ministry to another needs to be placed in the context of an understanding of the initial call to the ministry itself. Here we do not undertake a full theological analysis of calling but offer a few fundamental observations.

Pastors generally are honest in believing that they are called by God to ministry. Individuals may be honestly mistaken; the moving of God's Spirit is sometimes hard to discern. Nevertheless, we believe that most ministers struggle honestly with the question of calling.

The theology of call further affirms that the primary objective of God's call is God's people; God's calling of individuals is instrumental to the fulfillment of the calling of the church itself. The church, therefore, plays a crucial theological as well as practical role in the selection, nurturing, and educating, as well as formal ordination and placement of the clergy. A personal conviction of calling is expected to operate powerfully in candidates but is not sufficient in itself. The people of God always remain the matrix and mediator of individual calling.

Calling evokes obedience: the obedience of candidates for ministry and ordained clergy to God, the One on whose behalf the ministry is conducted and whose Word is the word of the clergy. There is a second obedience: that owed the ecclesiastical body within which the ministry is situated. The first obedience is unqualified: one obeys God, period. The second is essential but qualified: essential, because very few psychologically normal individuals presume to need no counsel from others pledged to serve God; and qualified, because as human mediators of the Word and counsel of God, advisory bodies may be wrong. When that is believed to have occurred, ministers must declare in all humility what they believe the divine Word to be and accept the consequences of prophetic testimony.

These theological and ethical categories affect the decisions and behavior of candidates for ministry and ordained clergy in ways intimately related to individual egoism, levels of emotion at moments of decision, traditions in congregations and denominations, and other human and historical conditions. This book is not the place for a psychological and social analysis of all the influences and inclinations that induce the young to choose clergy careers and the mature to persist in them or leave them. Professional ethical behavior must be hammered out in the midst of all the forces that affect each person. It is the duty of all concerned in the selection of the clergy to bring ethical understandings to bear on the human and social givens of the aspiring clergy. The continuing growth of professional personnel equally requires the motivating power of substantive ethical commitments.

Churches will and should decide by their own criteria and procedures who is acceptable as a candidate for ordination. Inevitably, church bodies will make mistakes about the sincerity of certain individuals and about their qualifications. Some callings point to lay functions, not clergy roles, and individuals and church bodies must make judgments on these choices.

Once in a pastorate, a minister may be called to a new place or a different function in ministry. Such a time of choosing may arise through an invitation or may arise from self-questioning. Would this congregation benefit from a new voice with a different perspective? Is my health adequate for the work? Can my family needs be met here? Is the Spirit working within these reflections or mere ambition? What are the ethical issues?

*Pastor G. was progressing well in his pastorate when his wife informed him that their marriage was ended and left him. The trauma that followed—guilt, loneliness, preoccupation—interfered with his work and he concluded that he must begin afresh in another location. An experienced inner-city pastor, he accepted a well-endowed but very run-down parish in the former gold coast section of a large midwestern city. The change helped him achieve a sense of new beginning in both his life and work and he was effective.*

Pastor G.'s decision to leave was not determined by the evolution of the parish he served—apart from the divorce, he might have continued there—or the development of his career, but by personal considerations. These vary widely and may include health problems, "burnout," lack of opportunity for gifted children or insufficient income to educate them, or a spouse's intense dislike of the community.

Pastor G. acted responsibly in recognizing that his work was harmed by his trauma and that the parish was affected. This concern correlated with his view that his own recovery called for a change of scene. His choice was not dictated by demoralization—he did not abandon the ministry in despair—but by a professional manner of thinking and serious reflection on his calling in a new life situation.

A decision for change may be made, of course, by other agencies: a congregation, a bishop, or a judicatory committee. Here, the ethical issue centers on the appropriate response. When a change is forced, there is danger that a clear view of the materials of calling—one's talents and vows, the best interest of the gospel, the good repute of the church—may be obscured by anger. Pastors who survive emotionally remain capable of deciding whether anger shall predominate or the event will awaken fresh thought on calling and powerfully impel a professional career.

Most changes of pastoral position follow an invitation from a church without an incumbent pastor. Especially when the congregation is larger, more interestingly populated and located, and particularly where the salary is higher and the prestige greater, a normal desire for advancement may carry all before it. However, there may be other motives less conspicuously related to career success. A congregation of similar size or smaller and with many problems may attract a pastor skilled in problem solving and rebuilding. The need for stimulus after success may induce a pastor to undertake a new church development instead of continuing in an established congregation.

Responsible decisions arise from a clear grasp of the ethical issues posed by choice, in fully realizing the ambiguities that are involved. Do the needs and demands of the proposed position correspond with one's capabilities, experience, and motivations? Candidates are not equally well prepared for every job. But the balance must be favorable to the change. Is the situation in one's own congregation such that a change of pastors can be made without excessively harmful effects? Might it be better for the church to have a new pastor? To what extent do the attractions of new location, salary, and prestige, if present, tend to prevent candid thought on the above questions?

Personal considerations cannot be neglected, such as the impact on one's family, the adequacy of one's health, financial planning for the education of children, or retirement preparations. A very responsible process is to list all the concerns relevant to a job change, evaluate them for their relative weight, and then determine the questions that are ethically the most difficult. If married, such an analysis should be shared with one's spouse. A trusted counselor can be helpful in achieving some objectivity in judgment.

A very serious problem for pastors in mainline denominations arises from declines in membership and a diminished number of congregations. There are fewer openings. Pastors who feel it is time to move may find no opportunity. Job change is difficult in lay occupations as well and persons facing a career impasse often feel great stress.

Some leave the pastoral ministry in these circumstances; others sink into a mood of quiet desperation. This is a problem for church executives and psychologists, but there are also ethical and spiritual dimensions. Meaningful ministry can be performed in almost any situation if the will to serve is strong. "I have learned, in whatever state I am, to be content" (Phil. 4:11). We do not sit in judgment on pastors who feel utterly blocked professionally and personally stultified. They should be helped by their churches with respect to placement and counseling. But if there is no job available, pastors may leave a clergy occupation for secular work. Just as seminaries receive many mature students changing from secular careers to the ministry, some clergy may change in the other direction.

Furthermore, under the best of circumstances it is possible that an individual's sense of vocation may call for a change of occupation. In general, it is important that such changes not be decided in the midst of trauma. Respect for a calling of God mediated by the church demands something better than a purely emotional reaction. Church professionals who are profoundly formed by faith in the activity of God in their lives will make career changes in the same theological and ethical context as they would change pastorates.

The question of "leaving the ministry" presents special ethical issues. When the phrase denotes simply a change from a pastoral position to church administration or another specialized role, it is misleading. The ministry is conducted from many vantage points: there are ministries of teaching, writing, counseling, and organizational leadership. Many ministries, such as medical missions, do not require clergy training or status at all. Most churches are forced, if only for legal reasons (pension entitlement, tax exemption) to limit the terms "ministry" and "clergy" in some pragmatic manner. Church bodies are being increasingly asked to recognize many unfamiliar occupations as ministries. Pilots in missionary aviation, for example, may be ordained but need not be; indisputably they are part of the ministry of their own religious organizations and may be supported by churches. The ordained who teach in a theological seminary may also teach religion in a state university—yet the Internal Revenue Service does not grant the same tax benefits to the employee of a state institution as to the employee of a church body. Is one a ministry and not the other?

The church reserves for itself the right to determine what is the ministry of the gospel. It expressly denies that right to government, while affirming the right of government to make its own judgments in the administration of law. Accordingly, many secular (i.e., nonchurchly) definitions of "ministry" function in society. An individual may "leave the ministry" in the view of secular authority without leaving it in the view of church or clergy.

Amid confusions of terminology and status, the regulative concept of calling remains uniquely the church's own. Whether church or state recognizes a specific occupation as ministry or not, individuals may know themselves called to work in the spirit and ethic of ministry. The church's most legitimate question is how to distinguish clergy from laity functionally; it is not to define ministry in an exclusive manner. A lay person may be as truly called as any ordained person to ministry—but one that does not require clergy training or status.

A career may move from lay occupation to the ministry or beyond the ordained ministry to an occupation that fulfills more fittingly the life-calling of an individual.

*Students at L___ Theological Seminary were sometimes bemused to learn that their professor of homiletics had once been a Shakespearean actor and then a pastor before becoming an instructor in seminary. Couldn't he make up his mind? Had he failed at a series of jobs? They learned when they came to know him that he was characterized by a growing and changing sense of his calling—and it was such growth that had brought him into the pastoral ministry at one point of his career and removed him from it later in favor of a calling then more appropriate and imperative.*

Such a career history belies the assumption, largely the product of the myth of the unfrocked priest, that anyone who once was but no longer is a minister and pastor must somehow have been unfit for the ministry. Against such assumptions is the freedom of God to direct the careers of God's professional servants in novel ways.

Ordained persons who change from the clergy role to a job that does not require clergy training or status should not feel themselves lost to calling or ministry even though they perform few or none of the usual duties of clergy. The definition of the clergy is essentially functional, not philosophical nor ontological and it is regrettable that ordained people in lay ministries sometimes feel excluded from ministry itself. Formal recognition of a lay ministry as part of the mission of the church is certainly not beyond the capabilities of a church governing body.

Persons who move from the ordained ministry to lay occupations move from the professional and ethical context of the clergy to another set of professional ethical expectations. These expectations may distinguish them from persons who confess no special obligation to Christ or the Christian community. To deal with the tension between the world and the gospel is part of the witness of God's lay people in secular environments. The ethic of profit, for example, may dictate the dismissal of highly paid personnel whose work can be performed as well by lower-paid executives; but the ethic of the Christian faith demands that managers take full account of the humanity of their employees and be sensitive to the requirements of justice. Within such tensions laity find their unique ministry.

Ethics for clergy is narrower than ministry and is specialized to the functions of the clergy. Those who leave the tasks commonly reserved for those called "clergy" do not abandon their ministry in the world and may actually enter spheres of responsibility infinitely more complex than the clergy life and career.

## Income, Money, Property

A common source of stress for church professionals is money: insufficient income, taxation, and financial campaigns. The historic standard for clergy income has been simply: "enough"—enough, that is, to relieve the pastor of worries about the necessities of life. But it is more complicated than that. Historically the clergy family has sought educational opportunity for its children and has generally produced offspring who deserve it. But with education costs increasing, "enough" to send three children through college and graduate school can be a great deal of money.

What is enough salary? Various denominational studies have been made; most assume, appropriately, that a single income must support a family. But many a minister's spouse is producing income sufficient to raise joint family earnings far above the average income in the congregation. Family incomes in two worker households, especially where both are professional, quickly exceed $50,000 annually.

Questions about money proliferate. What ethical issues arise around wide discrepancies between the highest and lowest paid pastors? Is there something wrong about an income package (salary, housing, health insurance, pension payments, travel allowance, continuing education allowance) higher than $40,000 (choose your own figure!) for a family of four? Because these questions touch church policy they raise problems of institutional and social ethics as well as personal ethics.

*Pastor R. was the minister of a congregation of 800 people. His wife could not work because of health problems; he had two children in college. His average salary-housing income for a four-year period was $22,000 and had increased at an average annual rate of about $1,000—during a period when inflation averaged 9%. His assistant, a recent seminary graduate, started at the minimum established by the judicatory: $17,000. The assistant's wife taught part-time, earning $9,000.*

*Pastor R.'s home had appreciated in value during the 1970s. Calculating his income if he were to retire, he discovered that if he were to sell the house, purchase something smaller, invest the balance, and claim his entitlements, he could increase his net income to $36,000. He retired, sold his house, and took part-time employment: his first year's income was $48,000. With the church budget relieved of pressure during the vacancy, his former assistant pressed for an increase in salary and was raised to $22,000. A senior pastor was subsequently called at a salary-housing package of $30,000.*

One may leap over the numerous questions of fairness and practical wisdom that can be sorted out of this example by considering two alternative proposals. First, all clergy should be salaried equally—that is, with differentials for dependents and variable cost of living supplements but with no reward system for accomplishments or seniority. The second option is that clergy receive no income for their work as pastors and gain their living from secular occupations. The second solution is common in the sects but is not at present a realistic means of servicing the highly developed institutional churches of America.[7]

It may be argued that the first option above is no more just than present practice, since many of the ablest go unrewarded now. In any case neither option is likely to be adopted by any major church group.

What many denominational judicatories have actually done is to fix minimum salary-housing stipends.

The existing competitive system in the United States (which is not typical, when Europe is taken into account) is simply historical. Within the limits of denominational politics, congregations reserve the right to fix their own terms of employment when they assume the responsibility for supporting their pastors. Most of the inequities in clergy salaries and allowances flow from such variables as the widely varying abilities of congregations to pay, their differing views of proper compensation, attitudes toward expenses and pension allowances, and educational supplements. A person who accepts the present system of distributed church authority does not have the right to censure practices that cannot be ameliorated without sacrifice of congregational autonomy. What may be appropriately demanded is modification of the accepted system to assure greater justice.

Connectional systems of church government may vest authority in regional groups to set minimum clergy compensation. More is sometimes expected of a judicatory than its grant of authority permits. Criticism that ignores constitutional limits on authority does not stand on firm ethical ground. On the other hand, a judicatory may possess authority to do more with regard to income equity than it chooses to do and so may be ethically negligent.

Beyond the minimum needed for professional effectiveness lies an inevitable problem in affluent societies: fairness. Before one can speak of fairness in distributing the benefits of affluence, one must ponder the fairness of affluence itself. Americans and Europeans enjoy such an abundance of goods that its fair distribution seems to them a question that stands on its own feet, but a Third World pastor will ask about the sources of affluence. Is it the result of hard work or of the exploitation of countries that lose wealth to the activities of foreign business? Whatever the justice of the myriad claims put forth in this debate, it is indisputable that the Western notion of minimal need for family life represents an ideal goal of many persons in the less-developed economies of the world. It follows that any conception of what measure of wealth a pastor or lay associate is entitled to keep for her or his own use will seem highly exploitative to those who believe it derives substantially from their own natural and human resources. This is particularly painful to those who see profitable foreign businesses built on minimal wages offering no security of employment and where health and pension benefits are unheard of. The problem of the fair distribution of wealth is real wherever affluence exists. Such discussion should never be uninformed by sensitivity to the larger shape of the problem of justice as perceived by the poor. At a minimum, affluence imposes a duty of sharing that is unique to those who enjoy it. It also requires that sharp questions of economic justice in relation to supplier nations should be raised through the church itself.

Affluence—wealth beyond what is needed to sustain healthful and humane life-style—makes possible a system of reward for the more able, thus raising the difficult issues of comparative evaluation of professionals, discrepancies of living costs in various areas of the country, and the differences in ability or willingness to reward excellence. Less objective factors include the extraordinary talent of some clergy for escalating their own salaries, skill at maintaining a favorable image sometimes unsupported by professional performance, and overall fitness for the profession.

Not all subjective factors are self-interested.

*Pastor T. had always based his ministry on a high sense of the sacredness of his calling, so when his church experienced difficulties raising the budget he volunteered to forgo a raise of salary. Some of his officers wanted to make a second appeal to the congregation but he demurred. An increase in mission giving was funded but not his salary raise. This same decision was repeated in later budget years. When he retired several years later the Pulpit Nominating Committee found that it could not compete for a pastor with the proper education and experience without raising the salary a full $10,000. The congregation approved and the salary scale was upgraded.*

Conscientious clergy often feel trapped between demands of the soul and decisions dictated by economic and institutional considerations. Pastor T. never paused to consider that his sacrificial choice would have the effect of putting the congregation at a disadvantage later. An act of profound vocational commitment may work injury to the long-term interest of a church while at the same time a congregation may be extraordinarily well served by just such a pastor.

The ethical dimensions of this situation were compounded by choices that hardly anyone in Pastor T.'s church had thought about: namely, its long-standing acceptance of the competitive salary system and its characteristic clergy income policy. Having accepted and/or adopted a competitive rather than a sacrificial clergy income policy, neither pastor nor elders should have opted for an ethic of sacrifice—the pastor's—

in the face of financial problems. Eventual return to the competitive ethic was inevitable, foreseeable, and unfair to the outgoing pastor in that his post-retirement income was permanently diminished.

We have stated that the competitive system of clergy compensation is simply historical in the United States, a derivative of its bent toward congregational freedom as against central direction. The prevailing system of church organization in any country is a given for those who minister within it but is not for that reason normative. Just as affluence itself must be questioned and not only its fair distribution, so the union of historical denominationalism with economic progress is open to question as a system. The ethical obligation of the clergy and laity concerned with compensation questions is not fulfilled in the achievement of some fairness within a specific denominational structure.

As the ecclesiastical economic system of affluent countries includes compensation above and beyond need alone, it also makes possible the accumulation of investments. What are the ethical issues here?

While some pension plans include housing for the retired, most clergy must provide for themselves at retirement and active ministers and church professionals should plan to own a home by the time they retire. Furthermore, a responsible projection of retirement income against costs of living may indicate that social security and pension income are insufficient to meet living costs, especially when expenditures appropriate to a retired professional are taken into account: for books and other cultural amenities. Important volunteer services—or activities like writing books—become possible at retirement, provided the retired are not forced to work to make ends meet.

> Pastor Q. had three talented children for whom he provided top quality education. In his fifties he suffered a health reverse and had to change from a church that paid him enough to cope with his educational expense to a smaller church that demanded—and paid— much less. A manse was provided. At sixty-one years of age, it dawned on him that he would soon retire with no house to live in. There then occurred a sudden growth in the neighborhood of the church. He found himself with a very difficult choice: He must risk his health once more by working longer hours to meet the increased opportunity for church growth or resign in favor of a younger pastor. But financially he could not resign. With considerable guilt, he determined to stay on until he was seventy.

A few clergy have talent as investors or may inherit money. The accumulation of an investment fund is in itself not at all unethical; the

117

measures taken to accomplish it, together with its effects, may be. Control of money is simply a stewardship responsibility. A central question for the clergy is whether money management, like any other nonclergy responsibility, distracts from vocation. Is one called to allocate time to managing wealth? Brokers are! Are ministers? How much time?

The potential for self-deceiving answers to the security question is enormous. To be in position to give up a job that makes demands that are ethically doubtful is a luxury not many enjoy. The criterion here is responsibility. Conscience can afford to be sensitive to every nuance of righteousness when its bearer is well heeled. Such persons cannot feel the cruel bind of Pastor Q. and may never wholly grasp the predicament of the modestly financed human beings that populate a parish. The degradation of unemployment and the desperate fear of failing to provide for those whom one loves must be experienced to be understood. Oppositely, a sense of being successful even when performing poorly can flourish in the garden of financial security.

Affluence challenges any Christian, particularly the person called to minister in the name of Christ, to accept risks and undertake tasks that would be imprudent or irresponsible in another. Financial independence, whether arising from personal wealth or a soundly funded retirement, bears with it ethical responsibilities that are unique. Have healthy and talented retirees the right to refuse service for which they are qualified? Is it ethical for the affluent clergy to follow the familiar capitalist dictum that principal should be continuously augmented by investment income? The ethic of stewardship, in short, reaches far more deeply into the life of the affluent, in or out of pastoral service, than of others.

## Gifts and Bequests

It is not unheard of among ministers to become expert in getting themselves into the wills of their parishioners.

*Pastor P. was a popular, enthusiastic, somewhat boyish person about whom many women felt immediately protective. He himself could not understand why anyone would doubt his word, refuse his wishes, or question his behavior. Those who differed from him were brushed aside and most left the church. It was noted by some that he spent considerable time with the wealthier women of the congregation but those who spoke of it were accused by Pastor P.'s friends of being untrusting and hypocritical. In the twelfth year of his pastorate one of the wealthier members died. When the will was probated an amount approximating a quarter million dollars was found to be willed to him. A few months later at the age of 52 he retired from the ministry.*

Not every minister who has inherited money from an admiring parishioner should be compared to Pastor P. But every minister should understand that delicate ethical questions surround the acceptance of large gifts of money and property from either the living or the dead.

Certain gifts to the clergy are less liable to corruption than the above example. A purse given at retirement by the whole congregation, the donors (and the amounts of their gifts) remaining anonymous, carries a minimal potential for corruption. At the opposite extreme is the exploitative personality whose acquisitive instinct never sleeps. The ministry is abundantly furnished with likable personalities such as Pastor P.'s. Happily, not all of them are as self-aggrandizing.

A pastor may be the beneficiary of a large gift without having lifted a finger, dropped a hint, or biased his ministry toward the wealthy in the least degree. The difference between the behavior that we recognize as unethical and fully ethical conduct lies in the intention of the pastor. Donors have the right to give or leave money to whomever they wish. A pastor or lay professional who has never solicited a gift or showed favor cannot be justly accused of exploitation. Ethical distinctions often lie beyond the reach of objective evaluation, falling into inscrutable areas such as intention, manipulation, and the many disguises of greed.

A workable guideline must be defined. Ministers may and do advise on the making of wills; they should never exploit that role to personal advantage. A bequest unknown to and unsuspected by the beneficiary is ethically clean. What is ethically unacceptable is that the pastors should deal in flattery and feigned intimacy in order to obtain benefit for themselves.

While some money-raising methods are inherently unethical, there are ways of presenting the needs of the church that do not manipulate potential donors.

*Pastor B. and his wife were good friends of two elderly members, a couple living very modestly. Just before his death, the husband asked Pastor B. to assist his wife to manage her affairs. After he died, she drew up a new will. She asked the pastor to permit her to designate him as executor and he agreed because there were neither children*

*nor any other logical choices. She gave Pastor B. a copy of her will.*
*The principal beneficiary was the church—more than 90% of the*
*prospective estate. She included bequests of $1,000 to each of three*
*people. He was one of them. He explained to her that this might be a*
*source of embarrassment to him but she persisted and the bequests*
*survived two further revisions of the will before her death.*

If Pastor B. had not learned of the bequest to him until after this
woman's death, the question would be ethically simpler: no problem.
Since he did know, should he have told her that if she included him
he would renounce the bequest and return the $1,000 to the estate?
Or is that more than ethics requires?

When the will was finally probated, the executor was no longer
pastor of the church on whose behalf he had secured this substantial
bequest. He made the customary charge for his services as executor,
accepted the $1,000, and spent it on the education of his grandchildren.

A useful ethical guideline is the following: pastors who have advised
in the framing of a will (and all the more, who are executors) should
not be among its beneficiaries. In circumstances where there is risk to
professional integrity, they should renounce a bequest if they find themselves included against their will.

It is generally unwise for a minister to agree to act as executor of an
estate, especially if there are kin who could—and may believe that they
should—execute the estate. Where there are no next of kin, pastors
may well make an exception to this general guideline. The ethical
question may be summarily settled in the negative if the time required
is so great as to intrude on ministry. Some of the objections that arise
in a case of active pastors do not arise when the pastors are retired.

Gifts and bequests to the clergy are not ethically objectionable if
never solicited, although an excessive number of them suggests solici-
tation. To assist in securing a trust officer or executor is appropriate
when it is clearly an aspect of pastoral care. The work of the minister
in the congregation must always be safeguarded.

# 7

# Professional Relationships among Ministers

The relationships of professionals, whether working alone or in staff teams, are regulated by ethical considerations beyond all terms of call or contract. If there is a single fundamental category that expresses the commitment of Christians to professional relationships it is caring: the caring of ministers for the people and the pastors' watchful caring for the growth and emotional well-being of their professional colleagues.

## The Pastor Working Alone

The pastorate can be a lonely job. "Who is pastor to the pastors?" is a question often heard. Clergy should get support and help from colleagues in ministry: bishops, church executives, friends in local ministeriums, conferences, continuing education programs, and relationships with close clergy friends. In this matter, we content ourselves with observing that it is a responsibility of clergy to minister to each other as well as to lay people as part of what it means to share the priesthood of all believers. We also believe that denominational bodies should provide pastoral care for pastors as well as specialized medical and psychological care after crises have fractured ministry.

A congregation that cannot afford specialized staff nevertheless expects its minister to be competent in a vast number of skills, usually more than are really possible for one person. The expectation of omnicompetence afflicts not only the clergy but also the laity. In the fields of law and medicine where there is more specialization, practitioners have a well-understood obligation to refer or consult with colleagues where a case calls for particular expertise. Such practices are recommended in ministry.

We have already proposed that in rare instances pastors may consider referring a new member prospect to another congregation. A more frequent situation is that a pastor may need to consult with another pastor or church professional. Most parish ministers are not as fully specialized as many doctors or lawyers but they do have particular experience that can be shared. From an ethical perspective, consultation is obligatory where the welfare of the church or person is at stake. Some pastors are abler than others in counseling, administration, and evangelism, for example. Ministry could be strengthened if there were more sharing of experience and expertise.

Denominations often provide staff specialists in the areas we have mentioned. A few pastors keep such services at arm's length. They may see such persons as promoters of bureaucratic programs that they question. But there is also a tendency for some to conceive of their ministries as private preserves—in effect, personal extensions of themselves. Offers of help may be seen as interference and suggestions for improvement as criticism. Purely personal reaction does not foster ministry, and if effective caring is the cardinal objective of ministry, any choice that impedes better pastoral care is unethical.

A counselee whose situation calls for professional psychological expertise should be referred to a psychotherapist who will make an independent evaluation. But when a case is not so severe as to require outright referral, another pastor may give crucial counsel to a colleague. In such consultation, when is trust betrayed? Pastors may be guided by the ethics of other professions, especially clinical psychology. It is proper to share information where such sharing is instrumental to the treatment of the patient. It is helpful to preserve anonymity, but in any event professional integrity is not a purely individual matter: confidentiality may be expected to prevail between professionals. A pastor consulted by another is bound to the strictest confidence in regard to information disclosed. Such a guideline is wholly consistent with the notion of the church as a caring community.

## Ministers of Neighboring Parishes: Sheep Stealing

Relationships with pastors and others in ministry at other congregations in one's parish area pose a series of problems. How far should one go in ministering to members of another congregation if asked? When does caring concern become sheep stealing? How does one determine if a person alienated from another parish and/or pastor really should be actively sought out and invited to join a more congenial congregation? What about really significant religious differences? Is it sheep stealing to evangelize among members of groups that deny the essentials of Christian faith? To put it bluntly, is an evangelizing pastor stealing Christian Scientists (or Seventh-Day Adventists or Jehovah's Witnesses or Unification Church members) from another sheepfold or bringing them into the kingdom of God?

> Pastor O. was asked by one of his members to call in a home where an aged mother was caring for her daughter, a very bright woman of forty confined to a wheelchair. They were very poor, did not attend their own church, and their pastor did not call.
> Pastor O. found the two women bemused by a web of practical problems and in need of someone to help them untangle it and make some decisions. The mother was afraid to spend the money necessary to solve some of the problems. She also demurred when the pastor offered to provide a lay member to help them work out solutions. He left wondering just how these folk could be helped.

Where individuals have rejected their own congregation and taken an initiative toward another, the pastor of the latter may offer his ministry as he would to anyone considering membership. This was not wholly true in the above case. Even though relationships between these women and their pastor were not strong, there was no open alienation nor had that pastor's opportunity to minister to them been wholly lost. Furthermore, the two women indicated no interest in changing congregations. So the pastor phoned his colleague, explained why he had called, and described the needs he found in the home. The response was tepid. The pastor concluded that it would nevertheless amount to sheep stealing to continue calling unless specifically asked by the two women. If they had stated that they no longer had significant ties with their congregation and taken definite initiatives, such as regular attendance at worship or specific inquiries about membership, the case would have been different.

The balance here is between professional responsibility to colleagues—for example, to do what one can to restore the confidence of members in their own pastor—and the fundamental goal of the ministry to serve those in need. To take the position that one may not render any pastoral service so long as persons are members of another congregation, no matter how estranged from it or neglected by its pastor(s), may be in conflict with the calling of a pastor. On the other hand, to seek to interest a person who is an active member of another congregation and well served by its pastor is unethical. One may visit in the role of friend but nothing more. There are cases where the matter is unclear: for example, where pastoral services are available but refused. Conversely, a member may be loyal to a congregation but neglected by the pastor. A responsible policy in that case is to render pastoral service on an *ad hoc* basis without any suggestion of a change of membership.

A related question has to do with pastoral relationships to households where one spouse is a member, the other not. Ministers should, without pressing in any way, establish friendly relations with the unaffiliated spouse. Where religious controversy troubles relations between husband and wife, the church professional should be guided by the member in handling visitation and pastoral service.

> *Pastor Q.'s member, an elderly woman, was married to a man who had long intimidated her. She asked that the pastor not call in the home. Little opportunity to visit her at all presented itself. The husband needed an operation of some gravity and the pastor took this occasion not to visit the husband, which she was expressly asked not to do, but to minister to the wife, her member. She sat with her during the operation and in those circumstances the wife confided in her in ways that opened new avenues to her ministry.*

There is little value and considerable risk of further alienation in using family suffering to put pressure on an unbelieving spouse.

> *Pastor R. was asked by one of his members to call in a home where a nine-year-old child was dying of cancer. The mother was of Lutheran background but not active in a congregation. The husband was not a believer and was savagely angry at what was happening. His wife was dealing with grief by returning to her faith. When Pastor R. arrived he found the mother pale and very tired, rocking the child who was moaning in pain. He asked that her husband join them. She explained that he was an unbeliever; but Pastor R. insisted and the man came downstairs. He did not sit down but moved constantly around the room, saying nothing. The pastor's conversation with the woman touched the fundamentals of her life situation but was disturbed by the presence of her husband. The visiting pastor subsequently asked the local Lutheran minister to visit the household.*

The pastor was mistaken in asking this troubled man to sit down to visit with him. He should have listened more closely to the mother of the dying child. It is in no way improper for the ministry to be offered only to those willing to accept it. Referral to a Lutheran pastor was appropriate in view of the woman's own background and her search for renewal of faith.

The question of evangelism versus sheep stealing—that is, how a pastor is to act toward persons whose commitment to Christ as Lord is truly questionable—goes to the most profound commitments and theological understandings of the clergy. Most pastors are prepared to admit that their own wisdom does not warrant the ready exclusion of adherents of other religions from the kingdom of Christ. At the same time, they know themselves called to summon everyone to allegiance to Christ above all others. In this matter in particular, ethical guidelines cannot be used to evade the responsibility of pastors for their own decisions. With that understood, the following can be said.

Wherever a life-style or a sectarian commitment is clearly harmful to an adherent, a pastor is warranted in pressing the claims of the new life in Christ. One might cite widely publicized examples of sects that deliberately alienate young devotees from their families. It is not sheep stealing to seek to inform confused youth of the moral nature of what they are doing and the questionable morality of the leaders they are following. At the same time, coercive methods such as the forced deprogramming of youth can clearly take no part in evangelism. Intervention through information and persuasion seeks to return the gifts of freedom and responsibility to youth who have yielded them or been deprived of them by exploitative sectarians.

The pastor who seeks to publish the message of the gospel in secular and non-Christian circles does not go beyond the bounds of ethical propriety. It does not constitute sheep stealing or any other impropriety to use the media to advocate one's faith; it is simply an exercise of religious freedom. Similarly, it is improper to deal with threats to one's congregation by trying to deprive a rival religionnaire of radio time, newspaper space, or freedom of assembly.[1] The ethical pastor never denies to anyone the free exercise of religious choice.

Professionally ethical behavior requires the most serious scrutiny of the teachings of marginally Christian groups as Seventh-Day Adventists; sects such as Christian Science, which draw on biblical sources without making the Bible's teachings central; and such religions as Mormonism that have historical roots in Judaism and Christianity but have adopted other sacred books and follow other prophets. If it is not responsible for physicians to dismiss out of hand unfamiliar medical customs such as acupuncture, herb remedies, and spiritual healing, neither is it responsible in Christian church professionals to operate from custom and prejudice when confronted by the unfamiliar.

Our main concern here is not with problems of evangelism but with the deliberate stealing of members from churches that represent the same gospel, the same Lord. This may happen even between congregations of the same denomination. We were impressed by a recent conversation with a pastor and people of a small town church that had been receiving applications for membership from persons wanting to transfer from declining inner city congregations. The church people were troubled. Should not these applicants stay where they were and help with the job of ministering in difficult situations? Membership could not be denied, but the small town Christians had discussed the issue with the new people. They certainly didn't want to profit from the difficulties of other congregations. This is the kind of ethical sensitivity that gives life to the church. The unchurched are the proper source of new members.

### Ethical Relationships within Staff Ministry

Particular ethical questions surround the relationships of staff colleagues, made more complex by differences of age, sex, and ecclesiastical and professional status among people who must work closely day by day.

Only too often young staff members complain that they receive little or no guidance from their seniors and many rarely see them privately. Senior pastors sometimes lack a clear conception of their responsibilities to their associates. Where specialists are hired to execute programs in their areas of expertise, many senior pastors are content simply to turn them loose.

Younger staff members, for their part, sometimes lack understanding of the structures and attitudes required for long-term, productive group ministry. When left to guess at the concepts that guide their senior colleagues, they inevitably go in directions that make sense to them but may not cohere with the ministry of the pastoral team as a whole. Young staff members may believe categorically that new is better. Senior pastors are sometimes baffled by the impermeability of new seminary graduates who may be highly individualistic and politically oriented.

A basic ethical problem in staff relations is that there is conflict between the concept of ministry as *diakonia*, which implies that a minister should be servant to others, and staff arrangements, which are hierarchical and grant one minister more authority than others. *Diakonia* calls at least for equality or "parity" among pastors, while staff arrangements may seem to imply that one pastor is *the* pastor. One evidence of hierarchy is the tradition in some churches that when a new senior pastor (usually the chief preacher) is called, other members of the staff should resign in order to allow the new senior to choose new associates if desired. The implication is that staff members are simply aides, even flunkeys, of *the* pastor.

We affirm the essential equality (parity) of ministers in regard to their calling. We also believe that carefully defined and pragmatic hierarchical ordering is compatible with essential parity. A word about Christian ethical concepts of love and justice is relevant here.

Love (*agape*) befits the servant concept. It puts God and neighbor before self; it seems at odds with hierarchical organization. Love is illustrated practically in immediate personal relationships (the family, the encounter between a Samaritan and a victimized traveler). Love stresses motivation more than results; it is willing to go to a cross. Its sense of community is spontaneous and voluntary, often with little regard to structure.

Justice relates more obviously and directly to staff arrangements. It is at home with more complex and structured associations. Love appeals to altruism in its concern for other persons; justice is more skeptical about human nature and emphasizes the need to defend others' rights and claims, some of which should be enforced by law. Justice is more concerned with what is realistically achievable. Like politics, it inclines toward "the art of the possible." It attempts to be rational by treating individual cases in terms of general principles and rules. We are more comfortable with the "relatively just" than the "relatively loving."

Nevertheless, in Christian ethics love and justice belong together and each influences the other. Consider this case:

> There are three children in a family, each with very different personalities. The loving parents want to do what is best for each one. Yet if treatment varies too much, the children will have a sense of injustice. "Why do you let Annie do that when you won't let me?" But one child is tractable, another rebellious. How can both be treated alike?

From this we can illustrate the two-sided relationship between love and justice. On the one side there are tensions. Love focuses on the individual differences and needs of each child while justice calls for treating them alike (following general rules). Love moves parents to put the welfare of the children above their own (*diakonia*); justice says parents should have authority over children (hierarchy). On the other hand, love and justice come together. For those we love we also want justice. Parents feel the claim of equal treatment; favoritism is unloving. Justice defends the freedom of the individual to be different. Love also acknowledges parental authority, while justice in turn sets limits on its exercise to keep it from becoming arbitrary or oppressive. The tensions are as much within love and justice as they are between the two.

Love needs to be expressed in forms consistent with justice. Justice teaches love to seek new forms of expression as changing personhood or situation may require. Parents may love their children ruinously unless the inequality of parent and young child yields to the parity of adults as the "child" matures. Many professionals exercise specific authority over pastors who are their peers in principle but not in the organization. The limitations on such exercise of authority in a constitutional organization express the parity of the clergy and protect the integrity of professional relationships.

Hierarchy is a structure primarily of justice, though motivated by love. Power is exercised within consensual and/or constitutional limits in order to accomplish the work of the church. Consent to and support for that exercise of power are ethically necessary whether its decisions please or not. Those who exercise power need to be mindful of justice—that is, the limits on their mandate—lest the possibility of love be destroyed.

As a regulator of power among peers, justice controls in two ways. It defines and enforces limits on authority. These may be stated in constitutions or bylaws, but they must be actively applied. Judicial branches exist in constitutional systems to examine whether an exercise of authority breaks with justice by ignoring constitutional or customary limits on power.

Justice functions best in the presence of common understandings among professionals. Not every exercise of authority rests on an explicit legal or constitutional base; it is acceptable because it is recognized as just. Hierarchical relations, however constitutionally correct, are troubled when the persons under authority feel it is unjustly exercised. Relationships within the local church staff are dependent on consent to justice.

Love and caring can be destroyed by the jealousies that threaten hierarchy. So justice is necessary to govern the exercise of authority. Sensitivity to their balanced application to professional relationships is a quality of professional maturity. Failure sets loose resentment, which negates both love and justice and degrades professionalism into mere politics.

The "ministry" of a congregation is the total loving and serving of all the people, however distant, whose lives are touched by its entire membership. The professional minister directs this activity in ways congenial to the denominational commitment to worship, belief, and action, consistent with the policies of the congregation, and responsive to the professional understandings of the ministers and other staff. The ministry is one, whether of the congregation together with pastor(s) or of the pastoral staff as a whole. Individual colleagues have their own callings and competencies, to be sure; but these do not constitute separate ministries or justify the isolation of one part of a church program from another.

The notion that each member of a staff possesses an independent ministry has mischievous consequences. Senior pastors may feel that they should not have to give periodic guidance to staff members whom they believe to be paid to know what they are doing. But this means that the senior pastor's work is not known to aides and itself becomes individualized. Moreover, by example this encourages associates to go their own ways. Politically minded assistants of any age or status may come to regard the group with which they work—shut-ins, member prospects, youth—as their "own" and even resent contact between other staff members and those whom they have psychologically possessed for themselves. Factions are attracted to such individuals and a pastoral group may find itself divided and unable to heal divisions in a congregation. There is no institutional solution to highly political behavior among clergy except a system of frequent pastoral change. Such a policy may well thrust evaluation of professional effectiveness into the background.

It is a responsibility of the pastoral leader to deal with divisive tendencies promptly and, if need be, institutionally; that is, by seeking the judgment of the church's official bodies. Delinquency in this responsibility risks the unity of the congregation and the effectiveness of its ministry and threatens the politicized clergy with failure.

## Responsibility of the Senior Pastor

The first responsibility of the senior pastor is to an effective ministry, not only in personal performance but also in the effectiveness of the professional pastoral group.

129

Here is a question of the senior pastor's ministry to other members of the staff. Failure to address problems in the behavior of other members of the staff threatens the ministry of the church. A minister of Christian education, for example, may work most of the time relatively independently. Yet if other members of the pastoral group and the lay committee on Christian education are not regularly informed of the pastor-educator's work or if that work is not competently performed, the ministry of the whole congregation is injured. The need of internal communication is self-evident.

It is less easy to deal with the intangible problem of the impact on the common ministry of differences of faith and life-style among colleagues. Differences are inevitable and can be creative, yet a senior pastor who excuses radical inconsistencies between professed faith and visible behavior, pleading tolerance or pluralism, may jeopardize the effectiveness of the ministry of all.

A senior pastor may be simply baffled by a colleague.

*Pastor A. ministered to a downtown congregation consisting almost entirely of retired people, some of them pastors and their wives. Because of the need for a ministry to youth, the governing body engaged a young man just graduated from seminary. He had unusual skills. He was a dramatist, had led youth groups during his internship, and was articulate and enthusiastic. Pastor A. had little previous experience in guiding a young colleague and simply told his new assistant to do whatever was needed to create a ministry to youth. The younger pastor was unfamiliar with reporting procedures and there were no regular staff meetings. Such structures as existed in the church were largely in the senior pastor's head. The younger man was likable, impulsive, gifted but not well organized, and had no experience working with a professional senior. Pastor A. never found any way to articulate his own conception of the church's ministry to his colleagues nor had he a personality capable of firmly directing the dynamic gifts of his new assistant. In frustration he discontinued contact altogether. The younger man involved himself with a drama group in the community. In the spring it was discovered that income was down—the younger man believed it was a pretense—and the position was cancelled. Thereafter Pastor A. hired only part-time pastors to assist him.*

Here is failure on every side. Pastor A. did not have the experience to recognize the type of assistant with whom he could work and he lacked both the personality and concepts to guide a young colleague. The young man himself lacked ability to conceptualize and present to his muddled senior pastor a ministry that he could execute successfully.

What is the responsibility of a pastor to a young colleague?

Pastors sometimes fantasize about a system of seminary training that not only teaches candidates the theological curriculum but also produces mature professionals. The prevalent practice of internship before graduation has helped. A pastor who feels particular hesitation about breaking in a new graduate should select only the more mature. Yet there is great talent available among inexperienced graduates. They are, inevitably, incomplete professionals.

In selecting or accepting an associate, there is an additional duty of pastoral responsibility that is as important as any service rendered to the members of the church. To be friend and mentor to young colleagues, to help them acquire the knowledge and skills of pastoral practice, and to grant willingly the time necessary are obligations of senior professionals.

A senior pastor is also head of staff. Leadership of a group in ministry is a larger matter than calendar coordination, policy review, and exchange of information. Other pastoral concerns may be less recognizable but necessary to deal with. Is there consistency of personal and social behavior with professed faith among the staff? Where marital, psychological, or intellectual difficulties exist, how are they being cared for? When there are clear breaches of professional behavior or personal ethics, how effectively is the head of the staff dealing with the problem?

To be both a caring pastor and senior administrator is not easy. To tell a junior member of the staff that she or he is not performing an assignment satisfactorily is clearly a responsibility of the head of staff, but it takes a gifted person to couch such a message pastorally. To back away from this responsibility is not ethically justified.

It is the responsibility of the senior pastor to deal promptly, personally, and as objectively as possible with staff behaviors that are inconsistent with the church's normative view of ministry. Furthermore, where personality problems such as moodiness and abrasiveness threaten the effectiveness of the group ministry, it is the responsibility of the senior pastor to act in order to maintain that ministry.

## Responsibility of Staff Members to One Another

The archetypal professional worked alone. Responsibilities were only to self, professional peers, and more diffusely, to the public served. In reality, a very high proportion of modern professionals work in teams or within vast organizational frameworks such as the civil service, universities or corporations.

For junior staff professionals the reality is complex. They report to a senior officer who usually is trained in the same profession, yet individual professional responsibility remains. For example, a pastor who is the recipient of a confidence has an obligation to the counsellee to maintain that confidence. For the professional working alone it is natural to say nothing. But what about responsibility to colleagues in a group ministry? In a church staff it often happens that more than one pastor is relating to an individual and the course of action proposed by one pastor is known by another to be potentially harmful. How is responsibility to the counsellee balanced with responsibility to a professional colleague? There may be little risk in disclosing information to a colleague, but that is not always the case. Nondisclosure itself may involve a risk.

*A family consisting of an elderly mother and her daughter attended church somewhat irregularly but with enough frequency to maintain pastoral service. The brother of the younger woman was a physician, and lived in a distant state. The daughter was emotionally disturbed, marginally able to live without institutional care. The mother was enfeebled. The brother called the pastor saying that his mother was being threatened by his sister. It was his opinion that his sister was insane and should be institutionalized. The pastor of the church visited the home, found the elderly mother uncommunicative and the younger woman dogmatic, very resentful of her brother's interventions. The pastor explored with her the possible value of psychiatric evaluation. She became indignant and discontinued her church attendance. It soon became known to the pastor that she had turned to another member of the church staff.*

The information involved in this pastoral relation was by its nature confidential. What ought the pastor communicate? Since he had been contacted by the young woman's brother, who was also a professional, the pastor called him and advised that only he was legally competent to act in the absence of his sister's consent. The pastor also talked to one colleague on the staff, sharing such information as might enable him to minister more effectively to the young woman.

Within a staff, it is often possible to develop bonds that permit frank sharing of confidential information in the interest of the person in need.

The governing principle is the welfare of the person. Yet it happens that some member of the pastoral staff may not have developed the self-discipline that must accompany shared confidence and cannot be trusted with certain information. Such a deficiency of professional competence should be dealt with by the senior pastor or, if that pastor is at fault, by a professional peer counselor or lay leader.

Lack of freedom to share confidential information within limits determined by the counsellee's interest is harmful to professional effectiveness. Disclosure of information for reasons other than the interest of the counsellee—for example, staff members who feel compelled to prove themselves "in the know"—can be fatal to professional effectiveness. There also exists an opposite tendency to withhold information in order to maintain an imagined advantage within the staff. Senior pastors should discuss thoroughly with the staff the issue of shared confidences.

The criteria that apply to the sharing of information between professionals apply also to other issues of professional collaboration: the unifying power of shared calling, maximum possible openness in professional relationships, the interest of the individuals in need, and concern for group effectiveness in ministry. Such criteria presuppose a clear understanding of the goals of the whole congregation and particular assignments of staff members. Trusting personal relationships and a clear *modus operandi* in ministry are also assumed.

## Responsibility of the Junior Professional

Many of the responsibilities of younger staff may be inferred from what has been said about the responsibility of the senior professional. If the staff leader establishes guidelines, junior members are responsible for understanding and applying them. Where guidelines require change, professional team members must say so to their senior pastor. The hierarchical relation and the peer relationship of all professionals must be balanced. Many Protestant churches affirm the parity of the ministry in principle yet build rigid hierarchical relations in practice. For example, junior professionals may hold their jobs at the sufferance of a senior official. Yet assertions of authority typical of hierarchical relationships in business or the military are inappropriate in professional relationships. The Christian ethos itself demands openness in work relationships and it behooves senior persons in professional group ministries to make it possible.

The younger professional needs to understand the accountabilities of the head of staff and behave supportively. This means informing one's superior of conditions that must be known in order to make appropriate decisions, advising on the basis of special training, and conveying the views of the members to the senior pastor. Once a decision is made, it is the responsibility of the staff to implement it, to interpret it to those affected, and to recommend adjustments that may be needed as the program develops.

The senior pastor is accountable. On this reality his authority is grounded. All effective organizations of any size have subordinate personnel who know more than the chief of staff in special areas of expertise, yet the head of staff is nevertheless responsible. The professionalism of subordinate personnel is significantly demonstrated by their response to this fact.

Differences of personality may exist within a staff. Yet professional behavior functions to effect the best possible decisions. Effectiveness in ministry of the whole pastoral group must be the prime professional motivation.

Preoccupation with personal advancement or self-image is unprofessional and the basis of much unethical behavior.

*Associate Pastor Bob was asked by his senior pastor to take responsibility for planning and conducting a seasonal series of services, inviting guest pastors known by the congregation. The senior pastor gave her associate certain guidelines developed through a decade of practice. There should be an overall theme for the series and sequential relationships developed among the weekly topics. The service should be liturgically unified, not structured differently each week. The associate pastor was asked to develop a proposal and discuss it with his senior pastor. The associate pastor was to conduct all services; the pastor proposed that each of them preach once and the other services use guest preachers. The senior pastor explained that she wished to review all services of worship conducted in the parish. Her guidelines for this series did not differ in principle from the usual style of worship.*

*Associate Pastor Bob developed a liturgy to be utilized in all services, and proposed themes and Scriptures for each of six services. This was reviewed in an early stage of development with the senior minister.*

*Some weeks later it came to the attention of the senior minister that none of the guest ministers had been asked to serve. Pastor Bob explained that on reflection he had decided to do all the services himself. Time having gone by, it was difficult to secure the services of guests. The members who attended the services were pleased by them and attendance was strong. The senior pastor was puzzled that her colleague had made a major shift in the agreed plan without consultation. She was left with the impression that Pastor Bob had made the planning of the services a means to claim personal control.*

It is not unusual that certain staff, some of them perhaps influenced by the social attitudes of the sixties and seventies and believing that power is the bottom line, should engage in manipulations of the sort here described. What is required in such a situation as this is frankness about what is really going on. If Pastor Bob was in fact seizing territory, certain fundamentals of ministry require discussion. Where does power ultimately reside in a church? What does "servanthood" mean in actual practice? How can a junior professional deal with authority problems? How can the senior pastor maintain order in the church while duly respecting professional colleagues? How can he/she function as a pastor to a colleague not yet professionally mature?

The incident here recounted may reflect fundamental differences of values. It is inevitable that some younger professionals should have concerns and make value assumptions that puzzle their seniors. The high sense of personal rights, for example, which has come into the forefront of American social thought during the last thirty years, arms young men and women with many new claims on their work environment. Pastor Bob in the above example might have assumed that he had the right to make changes without consultation. Where differences of value and personal formation exist, professionals have to work harder at communicating than the usual process for ironing out differences day by day.

## Popularity, Politics, and Professional Puberty

Most persons who join a church have a need not only to be loved but also to love—and the pastor is their natural target. Pastors are trusted by many before rational grounds for trust have had time to develop—a phenomenon that may be explained by an inward need of many people to believe in an exemplary person. Only too often ministers gratuitously loved naively come to believe themselves intrinsically lovable and entitled to "all the rights and privileges pertaining thereto," thus breeding thoroughly spoiled clergy.

One ethical issue for a minister loved undeservedly touches professional integrity. Certainly it is helpful to a minister to be likable, perhaps even lovable. But likability is not without risk. Ministers who are diligent in pastoral care are more likely to be loved than those who limit their role to public appearances. A reassuring personality can easily make its fortunate owner the best-loved among the ministers of the congregation. What begins as natural advantage—likability, an instinct for caring, disciplined work habits—may evolve into full-blown factional politics.

The only-too-loving lay members may have forgotten to give God the glory.

*Assistant Pastor L., approaching retirement, was assigned mainly to do calling because of the size of the congregation, the growth of the neighborhood, and health limitations under which his senior pastor labored. The latter preached most Sundays; the assistant had a month to prepare every sermon. Persons on whom he called sometimes made comparisons. Pastor L. was pleased that they found his sermons helpful but was puzzled about how to respond to the criticism members made about the senior pastor, whom he dearly loved and whose situation he understood.*

The choice of response here was complicated. The sermons of the senior pastor were rich in content but the style of delivery was constrained. The situation was open to exploitation. The assistant's negative options were unlimited, from knowing nods about the pastor's health, to suggestions that he himself was really holding things together, or to silent agreement that the preaching was a bit dull. Apart from the obvious ungenerosity and disloyalty of such responses, they all failed to seize the occasion to articulate the ministry of the church to the people.

The congregation needed to be taught really to listen, to look less for entertainment and more for solid instruction. Pastor L. had to remember that he was one voice in the total ministry of the church. The nuclear ethical question is: how can I respond so as to minister to every person involved?

If adulthood is distinguished by the intention and ability to behave responsibly, the passage from self-concern to a sense of group responsibility is professional puberty. Mature physicians refrain from conduct that harms the reputation of medicine itself; attorneys avoid practices that erode the credit of their profession; mature clergy persons do not knowingly bring discredit on the Lord they serve, the church, or their profession.

There is nothing sudden about the progression of human personhood from preoccupation with self alone to the enlarged understanding of selfhood that embraces the welfare of others. Many people, some of them professionals, never complete it. It is not a matter of one's age. We have all encountered practitioners whose single aim was self-aggrandizement in status and fortune. Such persons have never emerged from professional puberty. The faith and ethos peculiar to Christianity deny this self-centered way of life and work.

To describe professional development, we employ the metaphor of growth. Beginning with the natural self-centeredness of the child, human beings become increasingly capable of enlarged awareness. So it is with professional development. The mature professional of any age is not jealous of colleagues, does not politicize the pastoral task, or cultivate a personal constituency. The mature pastor has long since outgrown mere enjoyment of the exercise of power and simply accepts its responsibilities. Power, according to the gospel, belongs to Christ; ours is a stewardship. Mature staff people are not jealous of authority but they do expect it to be exercised in obedience to Christ. Between clergy essentially equal in calling and ordination and between ordained ministers and their lay associates, we do not speak of submission but of openness in communicating and respect for one another's calling, personhood, and responsibilities.

## Parish Ministers and the Nonparish Clergy

Among the worshipers seated before a parish minister on Sunday morning there may appear church executives, specialized clergy such as theological professors, retired clergy (including previous pastors of that very congregation), and theologically trained lay people. Some of these people's backgrounds may intimidate a minister. The problems that bedevil these relationships revolve around the polarity between the parity of the clergy and the expertise and even the power of the specialized clergy.

When clergy specialists choose a congregation they bring exceptional abilities to its total ministry, yet their presence may be threatening. Member-clergy (this term is simply descriptive) are able to assert themselves in the counsels of the congregation with special authority. Sensitivity is particularly important. It is an obligation of nonparish clergy to accept and reinforce the leadership of the pastor in the total task of executing the ministry of the congregation. When they discern problems, professionalism requires frank and confidential peer communication.

Member-clergy should not pretend to special authority in congregational life but set aside that quality in favor of common status with lay members. Respect for the pastor's call together with strict adherence to their own calls are the relevant principles. Love certainly invites and justice may demand that member-clergy volunteer for tasks where special competencies are required, like teaching functions or consulting on church process.

The above dicta apply to retired clergy as well. Effective pastoral care for them demands sensitivity to conditions peculiar to church professionals in retirement. These may include the retiree's need to perform caring activities within his/her health limitations. Retirement brings to some clergy a diminished sense of worth, which is not unique to clergy but can be very painful among men and women whose work has accustomed them to caring for others.

Retired pastors who remain active in the congregation or even live in the same city where they served sometimes pose a problem. There are social and psychological as well as professional and ethical dimensions. The protocol that retired ministers must leave the congregation and sever all contact with its members may seem unduly severe but at least it prevents insensitive retired clergy from hampering the ministry of their successors. An incoming pastor is necessarily new to the members and is entitled to the best possible opportunity to establish pastoral bonds and define a personal leadership style. Any word or action that intrudes on this right is unjust and therefore unethical. Commitment to the ministry itself demands that active retired pastors offer their successors every assistance, including absenting themselves. When sensitivity and judgment fail, senior church authority should move promptly to relieve the incoming pastor of the difficulties of dealing with an insensitive predecessor.

It is generally inadvisable for retiring pastors to remain in the congregation, simply because their level of involvement with parishioners is so high as to make the transfer of trust to a new pastor very difficult. It is best if the retiring pastor worships in another church.

The question often revolves around the psychological and social needs of retiring pastors. Are they harboring an anxiety lest their life's work be dismantled? Pastors who detect such anxieties within themselves should move away. What does the retired minister talk about with friends who remain members of the church? If there is any inclination to use such contacts to offer judgments on what is happening, the pastor should break these ties.

Another problem in relations of active pastors with retired or specialized clergy members in their congregation is that the active pastor may express anxiety by excluding worshiping clergy from functioning in the congregation or even by intimating that parish ministers live on the firing line and all others are strictly subordinate in dignity. Effective denials of parity in ministry, needless sacrifice of important skills, the refusal to deal candidly with personal insecurities—none of these can give rise to ethically strong decisions.

These counsels are not absolute. They are applications of the concepts of justice and love to examples of unprofessional behavior. Such applications may be formulated as rules, but rules are guidelines, not legalistic absolutes. There must also be an ethically sensitive judgment made about what may be loving and just in a particular case. Codes and rules used to defend oneself against criticism are poor substitutes for ethical reflection and sensitivity.

# 8

# The Ethics of a
# Worldly Church

Pastors face ethical problems that arise in the church's relationships and interaction with the world. If the church is in the world, the world is also in the church: the world of institutional structures and powers, values and goals, some of them at variance with Christian imperatives.

We cannot solve the problems of the encounter between church and world by insulating the church. Not only is it impracticable and self-deceiving, it is theologically faulty. God created the world; Christ died for it, not only for Christians. We are called to care about the world and live responsibly in it. History looks forward to the purging and renewing of the world according to the divine intention for all humankind and nature.

These are general commitments, however, and do not tell us precisely how to respond to the tension between church and world. We offer a biblical exposition of the relation of church and world as basis for the ethic we will subsequently develop.

## Theological Foundations

In its earliest era, the Christian church decided that God, known in God's promises and revelation in the history of God's earliest people, was an intrinsic part of the faith of those who follow the Messiah. The church rejected the view of Marcion of Sinope who set the New Testament against the Old, the God of Jesus Christ against the God of Moses.

A crucial section of the Old Testament is the witness of the prophets. What did the prophets teach?

> I hate, I despise your feasts,
> And I take no delight in your solemn assemblies.
> Even though you offer me your burnt offerings
>     and cereal offerings,
> I will not accept them. . . .
> Take away from me the noise of your songs;
> To the melody of your harps I will not listen.
> But let justice roll down like waters,
>     and righteousness like an everflowing stream.
>     Amos 5:21-24

Amos has seen that the accusations that Isaiah had lodged against the oppression of Hebrews by Sodom and Gomorrah applied equally to the Hebrews themselves. Isaiah had added that God wants us to:

> . . . learn to do good;
> seek justice, correct oppression;
> defend the fatherless, plead for the widow.
>     Isaiah 1:17

Amos insisted that while God was concerned about keeping Hebrew religion free of influences from foreign religious practices, God was equally concerned that in Israel, the poor were being ground in the dust and the needy were being sold for the price of a pair of shoes. Isaiah was concerned about those who monopolized the land, "adding field to field" until there was no room left for anyone else (Isa. 5:8). Perhaps Micah summarizes best the Old Testament thought on such matters:

> With what shall I come before the Lord . . .
> Shall I come before him with burnt offerings,
>     with calves a year old?
> Will the Lord be pleased with thousands of rams,
>     with ten thousands of rivers of oil?
> Shall I give my first-born for my transgression,
>     the fruit of my body for the sin of my soul?
> He has showed you, O man, what is good;
> And what does the Lord require of you
>     but to do justice,
>     and to love kindness,
>     and to walk humbly with your God?
>     Micah 6:6-8

Christians who reject the social witness of Christianity fail to recognize that the Old Testament concern for social justice is not rejected by the New Testament. Consider these words from the "magnificat" in Luke 1:51-53:

> He has shown strength with his arm,
>> he has scattered the proud in the imagination
>> of their heart,
>> he has put down the mighty from their thrones,
>> and exalted those of low degree;
>> he has filled the hungry with good things
>> and the rich he has sent empty away.

The Gospels testify to Jesus' reaffirmation of this understanding of God's will. The Pharisees and chief priests are held guilty of confining faith to religion and separating it from social justice. They threw widows out of their houses and then, "for a pretense, make long prayers" (Mark 12:40). They "tithe mint and dill and cummin" (going beyond the customary requirements of religious law; Matt. 23:23) but neglect the basic requirements of justice, mercy, and faith. They "cleanse the outside of the cup" but inside are "full of extortion and rapacity" (Matt. 23:25). In all of this, Jesus shares God's bias in favor of the poor, the oppressed, the outcasts, and even the sinners. "Truly, I say to you, the tax collectors and the harlots go into the kingdom of God before you" (Matt. 21:31b).

In the Old Testament we also learn that God acts in history. "History" here is not only church history or sacred history but must be understood as the whole of human history. By the time of Deutero-Isaiah, God is understood to be the God of all nations or peoples, not only of the Hebrews. God uses the Assyrians and Babylonians as the rod of God's anger. God calls Cyrus, King of Iran, to be an instrument of God's redemptive purposes. The covenant people of Israel are chosen to be "a light to the nations" (Isa. 42:6; 49:6), that is, to enlighten all peoples. Their position is not privilege but responsibility and they will suffer "double for all their sins" (Isa. 40:2). God's concern is with all humanity, not with a select group alone.

The prophets foresaw a time when God would bring about a just and merciful order of life. Apocalyptic literature envisioned this order as coming through a miraculous intervention of God. Jesus' own understanding of his ministry and mission was that God was acting in him to bring this new era. He saw it, however, as something that would take time like yeast leavening bread, salt lending its savor, a mustard seed growing into a tree. Still, it would rectify injustice and oppression.

> The Spirit of the Lord is upon me,
>> because he has anointed me to preach good news
>> to the poor.
> He has sent me to proclaim release to the captives,
>> and recovery of sight to the blind,
>> to set at liberty those who are oppressed,
>> to proclaim the acceptable year of the Lord.
>
> Luke 4:18-19

Like Israel, the new covenant community is to be a means of this work of God. The church is not an end in itself. To be sure, it is said to enjoy a "foretaste," a "downpayment" (*arrabon*) on the new life that God introduces into human history through Christ. The church also knows what God is doing; it has the gospel, the message. But it should not beguile itself with the notion that it is the only object of God's love or saving action. God's concern is for the world. The church's position, like Israel's, is not privilege but responsibility.

There are two respects in which the church differs from Israel as a people of God. First, with the Hebrews, church and state were coterminous; that is, the religious and political communities were identical. With Christianity in its beginnings, the faith community and the political community, the state, were distinct. The Roman emperor was not the Davidic king. Second, this meant that Christians could not depend upon the political ruler to enforce their notions of right and wrong, nor should they expect the church itself to exercise political power. The church's criterion was that "he who is greatest among you shall be your servant" (Matt. 23:11). God's power was manifest in the suffering love of Christ on the cross. Whatever may be said for the Constantinian establishment of Christianity and for the cultural achievements of the medieval church in the West, the state-established church cannot be the norm of Christian ethics.

This "separation of church and state" does not mean that Christians should separate their faith from the political and social life of the world. God's kingdom, God's new order germinating in the world, cannot be confined to any nation, party philosophy, or program, but it impinges upon all of them. Jesus did not reject zealotism on the ground that God's kingdom is socially or politically irrelevant.[1] He felt impelled (or called) to proclaim the purpose of God for all human society. The kingdom of God that he proclaimed embodied criteria by which any and every human social order must be evaluated, whether an existing system or a new order projected by reformers or revolutionaries.

As a teacher of such a kingdom, Jesus did challenge and threaten the social order of his time! And so he was crucified. He challenged the legalistic system of the Jewish culture and the presumed right-eousness of its leaders. He identified with the poor, the oppressed, the outcasts. He associated with women in public, treating them as equals. This was social outrage and a threat. While it did not directly challenge Roman rule, it threatened to disrupt peace and order in this corner of the Roman empire. The implications of Jesus' concept of the kingdom of God were later taken seriously in Rome and seen as subversive. It is regarded similarly in any society today.

Jesus' concern for the poor and humble is powerfully epitomized in the statement: "As you did it to one of the least of these my brethren, you did it to me" (Matt. 25:40). God's bias in favor of the poor, as we have called it, means not only that God is concerned about unjust distribution of wealth but also that God's love is bestowed on all re-gardless of human social distinctions. This equalitarian strain in the New Testament is reflected in another way in St. Paul's realization that the new community in Christ must rise above discriminatory differ-entiations between Jew and Greek, barbarian and Scythian, slave and free, male and female. The notion of "equal in God's sight" points toward Christian ethical commitments to human rights, freedoms, dig-nity, democratic processes, and to the relief of the plight of those who lack the material things necessary to a decent life. For discerning Chris-tians, such an understanding of the modern application of New Tes-tament teaching is in no way associated with privilege for the middle class, as charged by the Marxist polemic. Christians remain concerned with the injustices of contemporary democracies and their chronic inattention to poverty, ignorance, inequality, and prejudice. In many locales they are the most persistent critics of "bourgeois democracy." Unfortunately, Christians who deny the social dimension of Christ's teaching make the church vulnerable to charges of disregard for people excluded from a life of dignity by existing power structures.

How do the teachings of the prophets, Jesus, and the apostles affect our understanding of the interaction of church and world? And in particular, how do they govern the ethical conduct of the clergy?

The church should do its best with God's help to be the kind of community disclosed in Jesus' teaching of the kingdom. It has been noted, for instance, that while the early church did not attack slavery as an institution of the Roman world, it did effectively surmount the slave-free distinction in its own community life. But today when the church criticizes social evil, it often displays the same evils in its own life—salt that has lost its savor.

Early Christians lacked the means for effective social and political action. They were an insignificant group in a vast empire, which in any case was no democracy. In the United States today, by contrast, Christians enjoy access to political and economic influence and have responsibility to make use of them for ethical ends. It is wrong to do this solely in the church's selfish interest. The defense of freedom of religious belief and practice is an interest of justice and benefits others while it benefits the church.

In the light of biblical teaching we cannot say to people suffering political or economic injustice: "We want to save your souls; politics and economics are not our business." If we care about the world for which Christ died, we care about all that affects the people in it.

In the light of biblical teaching we cannot declare that worldly means are of themselves wrong as though, for example, Christians should not raise buildings or endowments to shelter worship and foster education. But the New Testament warns against our vulnerability to greed and pride, especially where wealth is concerned.

In short, if the church is properly in the world where God put us, the world of material and spiritual means is also in the church—because God put them there.

## Ethical Ambiguities of Institutionalism

Subject though it is to the limitations of any gathering of human beings, the church nevertheless is believed by its members to be a creation not of human art but of God. Its uniqueness consists in this, that it is the continuing embodiment of the living, dying, and rising Savior. His work is the basis of its ministry; his readiness to give himself over to death in order that we might live means that the church is supposed to be as ready to lose its life as any martyr. Christians are not called primarily to perpetuate their congregations and institutions but to be Christ's serving people, whatever that may require. The one concern of the institutional church is the ministry of its Lord, whatever changes may be demanded of it.

Yet candidness requires us to confess that while individuals often make sacrificial choices, institutions rarely do. There is a soulless quality about institutions. Persons may be merciful and humane but institutions lack moral sensibility. In a sense they cannot be blamed, since institutions tend to be more like machines than human beings. Those who have tried to humanize institutional behavior know how difficult it is. All this is sometimes true of churches and their typical institutions: boards, colleges, publishing houses.

Secular institutions do not feel guilt about their lack of compassion in the way that individuals do, even though individual members of them may. Organizations have other primary purposes such as profit or control. But this will not do for the church. As a modern institution it is still—and must be—the body of the Savior. Its only intention is to serve.

The problem of ethical behavior by institutions is epitomized by the rubric "the world in the church." The term "world" (kosmos) is used in the New Testament translations to denote both God's good creation and that particular sphere that the spirit of evil has invaded and corrupted. The kosmos in St. John is the total creation of God that Christ died to redeem (John 3:16f). The "spirit of the world," however, is a spirit of disobedience. St. Paul sometimes speaks of "the spirit of the age" (aion, often translated as "spirit of the world") and perhaps intentionally reserves kosmos for happier connotations. The "world" is present in the church in two ways: both as the God-given vehicle of its existence in history—faithful spirits housed in flesh, property for work and worship, funds for food and service—and also in the more sinister sense of the milieu of a continuing spirit of rebellion.

There can no more be a church without embodiment in gatherings of people possessing the instruments of active service than there can be a human personality without a body to house it. The "world in the church," like the human body itself, is not essentially evil; it is God's own created kosmos. But just as disease may take up residence in the human body depressing the mind and spirit, so the spirit of the age finds the "worldly" aspect of the church vulnerable to corruption and a ready avenue to the destruction of the work of the Spirit of God in the church.

*The Church of the Savior became self-supporting very quickly after its establishment at the end of the Second World War. Under Pastor H. it developed strong social programs. The physical plant grew apace with program development and the minister became as popular in the community as he was with his own members.*

*At the same time, certain attitudes began to develop in both pastor and congregation that were destined to mature into schism. So popular was the minister that persons who offered any criticism or even a suggestion for change were quickly told that if they didn't like the pastor, they could leave. A pastor's discretionary fund was established but never reported to the congregation on ground that it was confidential both as to source and expenditure. The pastor became interested in election to public office and certain members, along with some from outside the congregation, asked how the campaign expenses were to be paid, with pointed reference to the pastor's discretionary fund. Gifts to that fund were, of course, tax deductible under federal law.*

*The senior church judicatory perceived a risk of division in the congregation and asked for a confidential report on the pastor's use of the funds at his disposal. It was indignantly refused and the pastor attacked the judicatory with the support of his own committees and ruling board. The senior judicatory then suspended the governing board and placed the congregation under its own temporary governance as provided by the church constitution. At this, a majority of members withdrew, together with the minister, leaving a minority unable to support itself without assistance from the parent church body. At that time, the denomination was straining its resources to found new congregations in expanding residential areas and a decision had to be made: Should this wounded congregation be subsidized with funds that might be applied to new church development, or should it be closed to free funds for application to more promising ventures?*

Because God created the world as the residence of things spiritual, one cannot divide "world" from "spirit" rigidly. Still, we can name qualities that any congregation shares with other organizations that are clearly distinct from characteristics unique to the church. The "world" in this local church consisted of its buildings and money; its growth potential, both members and dollars; its organization and programs; its pastor's gifts and training; the morale of the people, particularly its pride in its success and resentment of criticism; and the congregation being prone to division. Any congregation shares all these properties with non-church associations.

According to Christian belief, the spirit of Christ in a church enters into all possessions and qualities shared with the world and subjects them to the purposes of God through the obedience of faithful people to the leading of God's Spirit. Senior church authority also possesses a worldly component, notably its authority to overrule the congregation's ordinary governing bodies. Yet it is responsible to exercise authority as a steward of God's own authority and may use authority only according to God's Word and purpose for God's people.

Let us be very clear: by "world" we do not mean to suggest that money or buildings or education or high morale are evil; we suggest that the world of property, funds, leadership, authority, and skill is in the church and belong in the church as the ordinary means by which the Spirit accomplishes God's mission in the world. All these worldly things are gifts of God, but because they are shared by all society, we are accustomed to their uses for purposes very different from God's intention in the church. Money is expended to build weapons to wage unjust wars. Property may house gambling establishments or worse. Leadership is required in criminal organizations and is often only too effective. The "spirit of the age" always invades the creation of God to carry the world away from its Lord. It is a responsibility of the church to return these gifts to godly uses, to employ them to bring the message of redemption precisely to those who have allowed the world to become the residence of an alien spirit.

Such statements may seem remote from the difficult practical choices of whether and when to intervene in a congregational division, but in fact the doctrines of faith provide specific guidance to ethical decision making. Where property houses not a community of witness but a quarreling crowd of people, senior authority must intervene with a view to restoring the community to its divine function and its property to God's intended uses.

Whether to subsidize this injured congregation or to apply the funds to new church development is difficult. Was there still a need for a congregation in that community? Was restoration possible? At what cost? Elders who were reluctant to ask for subsidy finally accepted the judgment of the senior church judicatory, and the decision to seek the restoration of the congregation became the ruling criterion of all subsequent decisions. Members who left after that point were limited to those who would not allow the issue of renewal to override concerns remaining from the past.

Let it be confessed with pain that in many situations there are no ethically unambiguous choices. Budding congregations deprived of support because of the cost of restoring the Church of the Savior were injured. A crucial ethical responsibility of leadership is to define a purpose capable of regulating and arbitrating among conflicting claims to limited resources—and to pray for forgiveness.

## Ethics of Fund-raising

Techniques for fund-raising dramatically pose the ethical issue of the world of money in the church.

*The Southminster Church of Esterton found that costs of repair to its 100-year-old sanctuary were prohibitive and decided to build on another site. A fund-raising firm recommended by its denomination was engaged and its methods explained. A select committee was to make a confidential analysis of the giving potential of every member based on credit records, income, and known resources. A figure reflecting ability to contribute was to be determined for each member. The campaign would follow Christmas and build on the theme "The Coming of the Savior." Literature featured the slogan: "God has no hands but our hands." The pastor was to announce her own pledge at the opening of the campaign, and was responsible for setting a sacrificial example.*

*A campaign of personal visitation specified that affluent members would be visited by persons in their own income brackets. Each such visitor would pledge an amount that would make the disclosure of her or his giving heavily influential in securing the goal decided by the committee. A follow-up program designed to catch stragglers was proposed.*

*When the pastor returned from the planning session and told her husband about it, he sighed and remarked: "Well, I guess if the church is going to have a new building, it's gotta do what it's gotta do."*

*The campaign opened with a stirring sermon by the pastor on the theme of "The Power of the Holy Spirit" and was followed by other sermons on themes such as the calling of the church and sacrificing for Christ. When the pledging target was reached there was a special service of praise and thanksgiving to God, followed by the systematic pursuit of laggard contributors.*

The ultimate effect of such campaigns on the spiritual life of a congregation is not everywhere the same. Some pastors dread building a church. Others report a net gain in congregational motivation. The tension lies between the extreme of faith that trusts the Lord while refusing all practical methodology and, conversely, sophisticated methods of manipulating human motivation so as to leave nothing to chance—or the Holy Spirit.

It is not ethically satisfactory to justify manipulative method by its effectiveness. The widow who put her last penny in the offering box in the Temple was not induced to do it by skillful manipulation of her guilt feelings. The ethical issue underlying the use of tested fund-raising methods in church life is not different from that which arises in the use of heavy promotional techniques for any purpose, whether fund-raising, membership recruitment, or influencing the community at large on matters of social concern to the church. God created the *kosmos* in the church: the intellectual and material resources of the people, their capacity to serve, their morale as a congregation. This divine origin must be respected in practice by strict adherence to the truth, not only factual truth but that subtle shape of truth that is communicated by the way facts are assembled and presented.

Where is the line between the hostile "spirit of the age" and respect for the "world" of God's creation? There is certainly a difference between simply asking for the means to meet need and the manipulation of people through evocation of guilt, stirring fears of social disapproval and presenting inducements that appeal to vanity and the like. All of these latter methods exhibit contempt for a believer's profession of faith. There is also a difference between a theological understanding of our dependence upon the grace of Christ for all that makes life possible, and a crass Pelagianism that suggests that the donor has the power to frustrate the divine will by refusing his hands to God's work. Obvious abuses cause campaigns to fail, but the unsophisticated are constantly exploited by manipulators who operate under the cover of religion.

The ethically competent should not find it difficult to distinguish cynical and exploitative measures from honest appeals to faith and faith's willingness to deal with the worldly needs of the church without embarrassment.

## "Tainted Money" and Conditional Giving

Those who raise money, including church officials, are sometimes confronted with the issue of "tainted money": that is, gifts of money of such doubtful origin that a church and clergy who accept it are morally compromised.

The term "tainted" usually means money accumulated illegally, as with the proceeds of crime. Some money originating in criminal activity is so well laundered that its taint may not be recognizable. Money may also be tainted because it was originally accumulated by means that have since been outlawed: for example, unfair labor practices or environmental pollution. Some businesses exploit human weaknesses in ways that are destructive in effect. Here we would list advertising that glamorizes use of alcohol and tobacco, pornography, the subtle perversions of sexuality in advertisements that pose alluring women beside autos and refrigerators (a practice that in itself demeans women as mere sex objects), sensationalistic news coverage that panders to a perverse interest in crime and violence or a morbid curiosity about others' suffering ("How did you feel as you watched your husband jump from the tenth-story window?"). In the world of business, practices may be legal but dehumanizing. There is concern about entirely legal business done with oppressive regimes abroad. What about profits from the international traffic in conventional arms and the all but indiscriminate sale of guns in the United States?

This kind of reasoning about the ethics of money puts us in a bind. Carried far enough, it can demonstrate that virtually all money is tainted. A church would not receive contributions from known criminal enterprises but it might well borrow to build a sanctuary from a bank accepting millions in deposits from a drug cartel. Does "laundering" make criminal money acceptable to the Christian conscience? We presume not. In most cases, churches are not aware of the sources of capital, whether they borrow it or solicit it as gifts.

Usually the connection of profit with wrongdoing is less direct than in outright criminal enterprises. A generous church person who is an executive of a diversified international business cannot possibly measure the moral quality of its far-flung transactions. Even less can a church know enough to take responsibility for the behavior of every person in the chain of transactions that lies behind the dollars given in good faith.

We must recognize that enterprises in any complex economy are integrated into a total system in such a way that all share both in the general profit and its moral defects. From a radical ethical perspective, the alternatives are complete detachment (which is possible only to individuals and sometimes very small communities) or revolution (which in practice may substitute the interests of one class for those of another—as, for example, in Mexico's decadent revolution).

Perhaps some attention to motives will help us decide. Money itself is not literally tainted; we speak metaphorically. Money itself is neutral, like fire. Its ethical significance lies in its uses and the motives that underlie those uses. Christians should question the motive of accumulating money (or status or power) when it disregards the cost to other people. One problem of accepting contributions from questionable sources is that we appear to give approval to wrong motives. The church itself can become so bewitched with the accumulation of the funds necessary to realize a desirable objective—a new sanctuary, a college endowment—as to become callous to the issues here under discussion.

A first step toward reasonably clean hands and a reasonably pure heart is taken when a church or church-related institution thinks through and publicly states its position on the decisions it most frequently must make. This will establish grounds for discouraging certain contributions. In the more complex and shadowy areas where the issues are not so clear, decisions can be left to the consciences of individual givers. The most disruptive question is whether the church should be involved at all in vast and expensive institutional commitments. The maintenance of these commitments obligates the churches to accept gifts from sources (or profits from businesses in which it has invested) that engage in practices that are at odds with the values of persons and communities whose first commitment is to Christ the Savior. The current controversy over divestment in South African business is only the most conspicuous illustration of this issue.

Here are some questions of motive. Is there any thought of purchasing salvation, atoning for guilt, or making something up to God? Money may be designated for a purpose that is unrelated to the purpose of the church, like the construction of an ecclesiastical mausoleum for the deceased members of a wealthy family. Some donors may use giving to force a congregation to control a pastor's preaching. In seeking funds, do church and clergy suppress the truth by allowing a misunderstanding or a misconceived hope or expectation to rest undisturbed? Accepting money, like asking for it, is a statement. One who has earned a salary claims: "I am entitled to this money. I did the work." A minister says: "My salary assures my freedom to work as God has called me." While a church accepting a gift cannot be held fully responsible for the actions of the donor nor the state of that person's conscience, it must state from the outset that its appeal for funds is directed solely to those who regard their possessions as a stewardship of God's things. It asks donors to affirm their responsibility to God and the institutions they support. Where there is substantial reason to doubt that gifts are made with this intention, a church may appoint one of its members to clarify its intention to a specific donor.

The quest for purity of hand and heart reminds us that there are no choices wholly free of moral taint in an integral society, whether we are speaking of politics or economics. It is proper to Christian life to seek the best way among the better and worse choices actually available, yet there is no way to live and serve in the world—nor to employ God's worldly gifts to God's people in the spirit of the gospel—that leaves no taint at all. We therefore live and act in prayer of confession and petition for forgiveness. All we can pray, finally, is: "Thy will be done on earth. . . ."

## Church Politics

There is nothing pejorative in the word "politics" if it represents the familiar dynamics of open organization and honest persuasion. But that is not what is usually connoted by "church politics." From democracy in mass society we have learned the uses of secrecy and surprise, appeals to vanity and greed, the uses of self-interest, and even "disinformation," a euphemism for lies. We reserve the word "statesman" for well-esteemed men and women in public life and apply the term "politician" to those skilled at the manipulative arts we call "politics." It was said of the late President Lyndon Johnson that he was able to put the Great Society program through Congress because he knew who every congressman was sleeping with. True or not, the statement articulates the undertone often intended by the word "politics."

How can such a thing as "church politics" then exist?

The entire biblical record dignifies group leadership and calls God's blessing upon it. Those chosen to rule the church were believed to be God's own choices (see Acts 1:23-26). Church politics stands on the beliefs that the divine Spirit is active among believers, that the obedient disciple seeks to know the divine will, and that God honors the covenant with God's people. In many polities, prayer is required before meetings of church bodies. The meaning of that practice is very far from the reason for public prayer in secular environments, as when the chaplain of the United States Senate offers prayer. The Senate contains believers but does not operate on the assumption that the senators are united by faith in a search for the way of God. The church does.

An ethical politics of church life is grounded in an honest search for the divine will in group life, full respect for the presence of God's Spirit in each believer, and refusal of manipulation of all sorts, including the manipulation of parliamentary order. Often believers communicate among themselves hoping to make decisions that reflect their developing sense of what God wants God's people to do and be. Such a caucus may be God's way as well as ours. Or it may not be! As with fund-raising, there must be fidelity to facts and their interpretation in ways that disclose the truth rather than manipulating them to mislead or misrepresent. There must be respect for the personhood of others. A so-called "church" populated by fools or knaves who really can be controlled by appeals to self-interest is no church, and its leaders are no ministers.

The political behavior of Christians is characterized by openness. Fellow believers seek aid from each other in discovering what God's servant-people should do. Lack of openness stifles the common prayer, the meaning of relevant facts, and the struggle to know God's way. Openness creates vulnerability but is so central to deliberation among Christians that the consequences of vulnerability are preferable to those of secrecy.

Perhaps the greatest obstacle to valid church politics is misunderstanding and fear of power and consequent failure of trust. Here again, the believer stands on different ground than the secular citizen. Power belongs to God, not the faction that can successfully seize it. Power is administered as a service to God, a stewardship that makes a believer tremble.

The human psyche is full of hang-ups about authority, much of it originating in unresolved relationships with parents, living and dead. And the public has so often been abused by the misuses of power that constitutional and legal limitations on it are necessary. There is no more painful example of the world in the church than the spectacle of a church official using secular political methods to obtain power for purposes that very few can believe truly serve God.

Power and authority are divine creations, part of the created *kosmos*. Yet they are corrupted when removed from the ethos of service. Public officials, not to speak of church officers and clergy, hold their authority from God and are his ministers as St. Paul stated in Romans 13. Power and authority in the church are manifestations of God's rights and Christ's power and authority to save.

How may the exercise of authority enhance the ministry of the church and confirm its character as the servant people of Christ?

*Pastor N. had shown himself a competent minister in several congregations and was a very effective participant in committee responsibilities. In middle life, long-repressed emotional forces broke the smooth surface of his marriage, indeed his very personality. He believed that he had been controlled by a wife skilled in manipulation and told her that he was through with the way of life she had imposed on him. She was dumbfounded, unable to recognize herself as described by her suddenly furious husband. He shared his decision for divorce with church authorities. She sought support in the congregation.*

*Within a few months the divorce had polarized the congregation. Numbers left, declaring they could no longer stomach the ministry of*

155

*such a man. After investigation, the senior judicatory intervened, notified the minister that he must resign and recommended that he seek counseling. He was offended but obeyed.*

Let it first be noted that the church judicatory used its authority very properly. Internal division had reduced the normal political order of this congregation to chaos, and the first use of higher authority is to restore the congregation to effective self-government. It is necessary to assure order if justice is to be served. Of course, church judicatories must take account of a variety of relevant criteria in forming judgments in such circumstances. What is fair to the couple in conflict or the claims of congregational factions? What does the church owe an ordained minister who has, in the view of some, gone off the track? How does the future of the congregation itself figure in decision making?

Ethically responsible thinking first determines the regulative criteria, both theological and ethical. The judicatory believed that this congregation was called to witness, unity, and mutual ministry within the membership. It further believed that it could not be reunified under the pastor because he could never recover the respect necessary to function as pastor to all the people of the congregation. It further believed that with counselling and an interval of time, the minister could resume effective ministry elsewhere. It did not attempt to make an independent judgment about the causes of the breakdown of his marriage.

The criteria of an appropriate church politics and the justification for the exercise of authority are the justice that understands and deals restoratively with human frailty and the love that always recalls the church to its reason for existing.

## The Ethic of Success

The word success, like the word politics, is laden with pejorative undertones. Success can be characterized as an idol that betrays its worshipers by corrupting their talent and despoiling them through greed and pride. Or the word can simply mean the achievement of goals.

*After ten years in the ministry, Pastor P. was called to the pastorate of a new church in a growing suburb. The judicatory and the nuclear congregation were in total agreement on goals: to build up the congregation by aggressive evangelism in the community, to organize and conduct programs as needed to serve the developing congregation,* and to care for the religious and personal needs of individuals through teaching and counseling.

The choice of the above goals and the criteria of Pastor P.'s success were dictated by certain assumptions: namely, that the congregation must become self-supporting within a reasonable time; that it required vigorous pastoral service in order to grow; that strong programs would be necessary to attract and hold families; and that a pastor must not be organizer and promoter at the expense of the cure of souls.

The circumstances of other churches call for different definitions of success.

Dr. D. was asked to become the pastor of a congregation that had been approved for redevelopment. Its buildings were situated in an area that had once been residential but now had the combined ingredients of small businesses, poor people surviving in minimal living conditions, racial tensions, unemployment, vagrancy, and uncertainty about the attitude of the city toward redevelopment of the area. Self-support had to be achieved within five years.

Despite his misgivings, Dr. D. accepted the call. His first task was to help the church define its goals more specifically. A growth goal had already been decided, the number chosen more on the basis of the financial support needed to achieve self-support than an evaluation of the church's probable effectiveness in outreach. Dr. D. persuaded the congregation to make a more thorough study.

The study was completed eight months later. It gave no reason to believe that the church would be able to achieve self-support in the foreseeable future. The church officers concluded that if the church were to remain in its location it must become a mission program of the judicatory; conversely, if self-support were to be the governing criterion of the decision, the congregation must close or rebuild in the suburbs.

Dr. D. was not surprised by the outcome of the study and put the choice before the sponsoring judicatory. After consultation with the church, a decision was made to relocate.

Dr. D. was disappointed. He was committed to ministry in the city and the very stubbornness of the problems had attracted him to the church. During the decision-making process he had hoped that the subsidizing judicatory might undertake a mission where his congregation was situated but he determined to see the church through its transition and later seek a pastorate in the city once more.

157

How does the experience of this pastor relate to the concept of success? Fortunately for his own peace of mind, Dr. D.'s approach to success was not entirely defined by the redevelopment goals of his church. He was a mature person whose professional standards were his own, whatever his job. To him, success lay in making an appropriate response to his circumstances.

It was essential to Dr. D.'s professional stance that the realities of the community and the role of the church in it be clarified; thus he insisted on a broader data base and a review of the decisions made before his coming. In that he succeeded. Professionals who share his standards would agree that he was successful. But it was a very limited success, however crucial to the church's future. Dr. D. found himself committed to a task that he had not chosen and would not have chosen, had he understood the situation when he took the job. His response was to follow through until the congregation had been freshly stabilized. If he had wanted quantitative success, he would have rejoiced at the decision since the new congregation gave him an opportunity to build it up to a point where anyone would be able to see that he had "taken something that amounted to nothing and made a church of it."

When the concept of success is informed by conventional criteria—size of congregation and budget, positive public image—contradictions may arise between ethically responsible ministry and pursuit of success.

*The Pineshore Church was located in an affluent city in an area where agriculture was heavily dependent upon migrant labor. Owners of orange groves, packing plants, and truck farming operations were among its members. Conditions among migrants were deplorable. Numerous investigations left no doubt that only concerted action by public authorities and private agencies could alleviate the situation.*

*Over the objection of most agricultural owners, the judicatory senior to Pineshore adopted a resolution urging local congregations to make migrants an object of ministry. Pineshore's lay leaders were very clear with their pastor; there was to be no "political agitation" of the issue in their church. Money might be solicited to support a local mission that sponsored worship, health care, food and clothing distribution. There was to be no contact with union organizers.*

*The pastor of Pineshore was regarded as very successful by her members, colleagues in the ministry, and the community. The church had grown, its mission giving had increased, and she was personally highly regarded. She also was strongly convinced that in the migrant issue the church was facing a test of its authenticity and integrity. In her view, the New Testament challenged the church to take the migrants seriously—that is, to try to remove the causes of disease and not merely bandage the sores—and she did not see how she could remain silent.*

If there is a problem at the heart of the issue of success in the church in our time, it lies in the discrepancy between a quantitative view of success and the purely qualitative notion of losing one's life—or risking an institution's unity and wealth—in order to save it for its true vocation. A pastor may or may not have the skill to persuade members to accept the New Testament requirement of identification with the poor. The issue may not lie with professional church leaders at all; there may be no openness at all to so revolutionary a change in the congregation's understanding of Christian faith and life. Competent and intuitive church professionals know how to respond in the moment of *kairos* but they do not pretend to control it.

The mature church professional is moved by an inward and religiously formed concept of success. A clash between such commitments and popular criteria of success is intrinsic to a professional career in the church. To accept the authority of popular criteria of success is to surrender the professional self. The effects of this are particularly devastating to those who take ordination vows, since the meaning of success in a pervasively secularized culture is inevitably remote from the notion of discipleship. God and God's ministers have a controversy with the secular world, as the American Puritans might have expressed it. All church professionals must be highly autonomous in relation to modern society. Autonomy for us means personally to choose a Lord who stands at every moment in the starkest contrast to the authorities that shape the "spirit of the age."

Professional servants of the church should know how to live with success. How much stock do we take in quantitative success? The answer has got to be: "not much." Are those people coming to church to honor Christ or are they merely responding to the rhetorical skills or personal charms of their pastor or youth leader? Who can say with any assurance? Which of the numerous enterprises that make up any large church program enjoy priority in the pastor's allocation of time? Those that make for visible success or those where the quality of the pastoral office is tested? What does your salary mean to you? Does it testify authoritatively that you are successful? Or does a below-average salary testify to your failure, or perhaps your holiness?

Where the concept of success rules, the cruel notion of failure is not far away. Is there an ethic of failure?

If you find it credible, the most ingenious way of coping with failure is to christen it success and anoint yourself with the rest of the oil. The notion of sacrifice can be manipulated very handily even when the cause of the problem is unprofessional behavior, such as laziness or incompetence.

But there are career catastrophes in professional life. Are they all alike failures?

*After having worked in her new job for six months, Pastor R. discovered that the church had become habituated to overspending its budget and had a number of commercial loans outstanding. She found that no plans had been formulated for paying them off or even bringing the budget into line with income. Although she reflected grimly that those who had hired her had substantially misrepresented the job by concealing all this, she felt she must make the correction of this overspending an early priority.*

*After consulting with committee chairpersons, she recommended staff and program reductions that would halt the overspending. She then proposed that a special campaign for funds to liquidate the debts be conducted on the basis of a frank disclosure to the congregation of what had been happening and how the church's future might be opened in a fresh way by an immediate and responsible dealing with the indebtedness.*

*Pastor R. had put her hand into a hornet's nest. Certain staff members affected by her proposed economies had their own constituencies: the governing board of the church had become accustomed to secrecy in its conduct of financial affairs and her proposal would gravely embarrass several of the church's most reputable members.*

*Her competence was called into question by several church leaders whose reputations with her senior judicatory were strong. She found herself on the defensive and decided to resign. Before doing so, she laid before her judicatory the financial problem of her church and urged that no successor be elected until the issues that she had not been able to resolve were settled.*

Responsible professionals, whether the victims of such a "failure" or among those called upon to adjudicate it, will be slow to speak of failure when in reality previous "successful" pastors had evaded—and aggravated—the problem.

Pastor R. might have proceeded more cautiously, to be sure. Had she possessed more sensitively tuned political skills, she might have timed her approach better and brought it off without disaster to herself. What needed to be done was really a responsibility of those who had long been there, including the higher judicatory; a newly installed pastor was hardly positioned to deal with the problem. She might have been wiser to have clarified the problem before proposing a solution at the outset. But those are primarily issues of prudence and only secondarily of ethics. These are not unrelated: rashness can be irresponsible. But where an honest professional undertakes a course of action that fails, little or no question of unethical behavior need exist. Inability to foresee an outcome is not an ethical deficiency *per se*. The question on which the ethical issue turns is whether Pastor R.'s response to the facts she found after taking the job fostered the ministry of the church by opening the way to the resolution of problems. If it did, however costly to her, she cannot be called a failure.

Like success, failure often cannot be confidently identified in the moment of its occurrence. Events counted as failure, including the destruction of a career, may be a necessary suffering without which an institution cannot be restored. Even if mature professionals are hesitant to justify themselves by quickly evoking the model of the cross, the fact remains that in some circumstances a professional "failure" may be God's way of bringing the church to its senses.

# 9

## Ministers and Social Establishments

Relations with government represent only the most conspicuous of the "powers" of the world with which church officers, ordained and lay, must deal. There is, for example, the public education system, most notably the primary and secondary schools in every community. Other secular institutions in modern society are the professions, business corporations and societies, and a broad range of persons, now considered professionals along with doctors, lawyers, and clergy: dentists, journalists, accountants, veterinarians, social workers, psychologists, architects, engineers, city planners, and consultants of all kinds.

There are also vast secular philanthropic establishments in many countries, for example, the United Way in the United States. St. Paul's term "principalities and powers" might be applied to these in the aggregate, except that he includes also spiritual powers such as the forces of the mind that cause people to believe in magic, idols, and social and philosophical dogmas. Beyond all organized social institutions are obscure processes that we call "changing climates of opinion" or "new awareness." These are invisible and diffuse, often eluding accurate description or even detection in their early stages. All these taken together are the "principalities and powers," the visible and invisible establishment within which Christians and their leaders must live.

A responsible relationship to established social power involves an understanding of how the society functions, where its centers of power lie, and above all a very clear grasp of one's own calling and professional commitments. The church intersects with social establishments, but what are the professional obligations of ministers to both church and society at the points where ministers are engaged with the social establishments?

## Relating Ethically to Government

This writer recalls hearing from a Scottish minister at an international meeting an eloquent defense of clericalism based on an analogy between Christ the King and his servants, the clergy, who are to rule on his behalf. The Scottish pastor's tradition speaks of the "threefold office of Christ" as prophet, priest, and king, each office obtaining meaning from Christ's unique calling to be our Savior. But to argue that the clergy are to dominate modern society as Christ is expected to rule humankind at the consummation of the age is gratuitous and arrogant. It is theologically irresponsible to neglect the context of John Calvin's exposition of Christ as king: namely, that he is the crucified Lord whose victory lay in his very dying and who now calls upon his church and clergy to die with him for the salvation of the world.

Nowhere does the New Testament propose that the world be saved by conferring civil authority upon either church or clergy. It is in stillness and human weakness, in the persuasions of the foolish of this world and among the victims in any society that the gospel is first heard and received. It was a Palestinian establishment of religion and the Roman state that connived to crucify Jesus. Church and clergy are called to proclaim the kingship of Christ in his living, present kingdom. They do not seek earthly power nor manipulate law to the advantage of religion.

*At a conference on religious liberty the following problem was posed by a troubled clergyperson. His parish had been aggressively invaded by the members of the Unification Church and several of the church's youth had broken ties with both family and church and gone to live in a commune in obedience to the Reverend Moon.*

*The commune was in violation of several local laws regarding zoning, sanitation, and overcrowding. These laws, the minister pointed out, were purely secular and applied equally to all. If found in violation, the commune could be closed up. He argued that no violation of religious freedom would be involved in aggressive prosecution because the relevant law was secular; but its principal effect would be to relieve the church and community of the Unification Church.*

The conference leader responded categorically: any such legal action, even though constitutional, represents manipulation of law for religious purposes and would damage both religious freedom and the integrity of religion itself.

The question here is whether the constitutional and legal use of governmental power by some religious groups to achieve their desires is ethical. Models for the clergy come from the offices of Christ as prophet and priest.

The church and its ministry are nothing if not the prophets and apostles of Christ. A prophet is a truth-teller; prophet and apostle tell the truth of the saving work of God through God's Son. There is always conflict between the establishments of human society and the prophetic Word of God. The church and its professionals stand at the intersection of this conflict.

The church itself has a double character. It is an institution of society and its professionals are leaders of an ecclesiastical establishment. At the same time the church is the worshiping body of Christ and the pastors are his priests and teachers. The social form of the church varies from tiny groups with neither property nor professional leadership to established churches with vast institutions, properties, and social impact. Regardless of its social form, the church is a worshiping community and is defined and regulated by the gifts of the unchanging Christ.

The ethic of the church's professional leaders is grounded in the gifts of Christ, whatever the institutional form or social role of clergy. The conduct of a minister is substantially influenced by the form of the church in each time and place. No church ever achieved historical existence without some degree of institutionalization and no institutional church is truly a church once it has ceased to be the recipient of Christ's gifts.

One of the gifts of Christ is authority. He has granted one authority to the state, another to the church. The ministry of the church and its ministers require them to speak of all the divine gifts, including the duties of government and the limits God has placed on it, and to respect all of God's gifts and the boundaries that separate them.

One such address of church to state is found in a Presbyterian declaration of 1787.

> God alone is lord of the conscience and hath left it free from the doctrine and commandment of men; which are many times contrary to his Word. . . . Therefore they consider the rights of private judgment, in all matters that respect religion as universal and unalienable. . . ."[1]

165

The state will never be immune from the criticism of its citizens, including criticism based on religious values. Both church and clergy are within proper limits in addressing civil concerns on moral and religious grounds.

Most actions or speech concerning state and society in regard to social change are ambiguous. In defending religious liberty, for example, church and clergy usually claim as the right of religion such practical advantages as exemption from taxation of church property on ground that taxation adds to the burden of the practice of religion and may even be used to destroy it, which the state may not do. Civil and religious liberty are also essential to the integrity of faith and conscience. Thus in matters of tax exemption of church property and civil liberty, the church is both defending its rights and obtaining some advantage to itself. Such ambiguity can be endured only insofar as the church devotes all it possesses to the humble service of its Lord.

While the clergy defends the liberties of religion, it must at the same time speak prophetically to society and has the moral and civil right to do that. One of the risks of tax exemption is that it may be perceived not as a right but as a privilege subject to annulment if the church speaks too critically to the state. Those who have calculated the cost of paying property taxes know the scale of the exposure created by religious tax exemption. Believers are committed to be a prophetic people and they struggle with the ambiguities between constitutional rights and the advantages and risks of exemptions.

The priestly role of the clergy, when considered in relation to the church's situation in secular society, is complex. Its priesthood is Christ's own priesthood or it is nothing. He alone is the mediator of salvation to humankind. Insofar as the clergy are priests, they are duly ordained teachers and administrators of Christ's own gifts. They administer the sacraments, teach the Word, and lead the church in worship and Christian action. The priestly role of the ordained is purely a matter of faith and worship.

The clergy is not called to a priesthood on behalf of secular society or the state. To be sure, clergy may play a significant role in the secular society as community leaders, even elected officials. They are not on that account, however, society's priests or even the church's priests to the society, as though God's gifts could be mediated by a secular priesthood working outside a believing community. Even when the whole civil community is united in profession of a single religion, the clergy's role in public life is not priestly. The civil community itself is not a community of faith or worship.

How are the clergy's prayers, for example, to be understood when offered at secular gatherings?

*Pastor S. was elected to the board of the local Red Cross Chapter. The board's experience with the clergy led it to expect him to leave the management of its affairs largely to the business people on the board. He was expected to lead in prayer at its meetings.*

*Pastor S. found himself more comfortable, in reality, with the management and budget problems of the Red Cross than his role as its offerer of public prayer. Was he functioning as some sort of secular priest? Were his prayers offered on behalf of the Red Cross chapter, as though it were a church? Was he fostering misunderstanding of both prayer and his professional character?*

These questions are even more sharply posed when prayer is offered at a governmental function: the opening of a legislative session, a patriotic celebration, a party meeting. Are ethical issues raised when the clergy offers public prayer outside the community of faith?

Some unexpected options must be considered. If in fact the clergy is understood to be offering prayer on behalf of a political gathering (in the way that the minister is the voice of a congregation in public prayer at worship), ministers give some ground to suppose that they regard a secular gathering as at the same time a religious body. Is this to tell the truth?

How is the clergy to respond to the religious strain that runs through the secular community?

*Dr. L. had been ordained in his twenties but spent most of his career in a state university. On one occasion he accompanied a delegation of students to a meeting of the board of the university to assist in a presentation. At the opening of the meeting the chairman of the board asked one of its members, a prominent Episcopal bishop, to offer prayer. Several of the students were Jewish. They were not so much offended as astonished. "I thought such things disappeared with the nineteenth century!" one said to Dr. L. He explained that the university had been founded by a church group and had subsequently become secular, but that it retained many customs of its earlier years.*

The board of this university included many who did not share the bishop's faith but they did not object to innocuous Christian traditions. Is there an ethical issue in fostering prayer simply as custom in an otherwise secular environment?

While church and clergy cannot assume responsibility for what people hear, they are responsible for telling the truth. This means not only getting the words right but saying them in contexts that make for understanding rather than risking misunderstanding or making misunderstanding virtually certain, and by acting in ways that are consistent with the theological understandings that undergird prayer.

While each minister must act responsibly, certain guidelines can be offered:

—There is no point in prayer that merely perpetuates custom, or is simply innocuous.

—Acts of public prayer are not liturgical; such prayer happens only in a believing community.

—Where there is agreement among religiously diversified groups, each person asked to offer prayer should do so according to her or his own tradition. Clergy do well to foster this practice. In this context, prayers may articulate the hope of a believing community for the meetings they bless. For the rest, they are kerygmatic; that is, in the nature of witness. Whether any witness actually occurs will depend not only on what is actually said but also on the role the clergy person has established in church and community and what the speaker is known to represent. Kerygma is a work of the Spirit through an obedient ministry.

—Prayers that carefully eliminate all reference to Christ in deference to non-Christian sensibilities are ordinarily not the best expedient. Still, some pastors find the practice justifiable in specific circumstances.

*The local high school followed the custom of inviting clergy to take turns offering invocation and benediction at commencement. On two occasions Christian clergy had given prayers that were so particularly Christian that non-Christians were offended. After ineffective protests to the school board, the case was taken to the courts. The school board had promised meanwhile that only nonsectarian prayers would be offered. The courts upheld this practice.*

*Pastor N. had joined the protests but now felt she should not boycott public school affairs. Among other things, if clergy did not participate, what sorts of prayers would be offered? She felt that prayer addressed to God but omitting "in the name of Christ" could have Christian content, and that the risk of misunderstanding would be at least partly compensated by the witness she had been making in church and community. When her turn came, she took it.*

Pastor N. was certainly right in believing that even without specific ascription, prayer can contain elements that may be wholly uncongenial to a secular audience. At a patriotic festival a minister may ask God to forgive America for its sins in Vietnam. A chaplain may ask God to cleanse the nation of greed on the day a legislature votes on a heavily lobbied tax proposal. Mere cleverness, not to speak of an intention to irritate, is not to be confused with courage, much less with kerygmatic ministry. At the same time, there are moments when prayer can break through in ways as unexpected to the clergy as to the secular audience.

Most to be avoided is public prayer that will almost surely be understood as an act of secular priesthood. Such occasions may be identified by their explicit or implicit untruthfulness. Is mere nationalism or chauvinism in fact reinforced by a public prayer? Is God's word of chastening left unmentioned in public prayer? Does the pastor's total relation to the public community convey the message that the prayer is no more than a priestly intercession? The question of the ethics of public prayer reaches ultimately to the largest questions of the quality of the ministry of Christ in the community.

## Public Education and the Civil Religion

In any pluralistic society, special questions are posed by the participation of church officials in sensitive areas of public life such as public education.

> Pastor B. was a respected member of the school board. A petition of a group of parents came before the board, asking that time be provided in the classroom for silent prayer. Their feeling was that all would benefit, whether they prayed or not, because the practice would foster respect for God. It was not proposed that any specific prayer be used but the period was to be understood as a time for prayer.
>
> Pastor B. opposed the proposal. She felt that prayer, unlike eating and sleeping, is not something everyone knows how to do without instruction. Young people need to be taught to pray and the public schools could not do that. Second, she believed that prayer should remain in the sphere of churches and families. She also believed that there are better ways for public schools to teach respect for religious traditions: for example, by including in the teaching of American history some information about the religions of the immigrants and about the churches, synagogues, and colleges they founded. She felt

*that the principal defect of the parents' proposal was that it posed a danger to religion: namely, of shallowness and misunderstanding of prayer.*

Whether as a member of a school board or simply as one sharing in the shaping of public sentiment, an ethical church official, clergy or lay, does not seek the aid of public institutions or public funds for religious purposes. No pastor is willing to permit the state to assume sponsorship or custody of religion or to intrude on the freedom of the churches.

Local school boards may be open to proposals for the teaching of religion in the schools without compensation and clergy may be asked to do the instruction. The fact that the work is uncompensated answers only one problem. Where compulsory school laws account for the presence of the students, it is improper to teach religion in ways that advocate the beliefs and ethos of a particular religious group, even though students in the class may adhere to that faith. In any school, religion may be taught historically and/or philosophically and its documents taught as literature, without constitutional or ethical objection.

Beyond these issues lies the debatable concept of a "civil religion." Justice William O. Douglas once wrote in a Supreme Court opinion: "We are a religious people." Where religion is taught in public institutions, at least one commitment of the society is expressed: namely, that it is better for the people of the nation to know its religious heritage than to be ignorant of it. Implicit in almost all teaching of religion is a high evaluation of the ethical qualities of personal and institutional life, whatever the diversity of faiths. Furthermore, it is highly likely that the motivation and instructional practice of the teacher of religion will convey an ethos that postulates a Supreme Being, moral laws that regulate the relativisms of human opinion, and a sense of structure in human affairs. One is dealing here, if not with consensual religion, at least with broadly consensual morals. Those who advocate the teaching of religion in public institutions are unavoidably entangled in the issue sometimes called the "civil religion."

There have been numerous efforts by American scholars to define a civil religion possessed of doctrines and moral precepts on which all citizens might agree and which therefore could be proposed for inclusion in public education. Such a body of religious instruction would have to be acceptable to all the varied publics, religious, sectarian, and non-religious in the American population. By definition, it would be "secular."

There is an important distinction between such a formalized civil religion and free student response to competent instruction in the actual religions that are professed by their fellow citizens and others. We take the view that in a context of historical instruction, it is ethical and constitutional to teach the actual beliefs and behaviors that are generally deemed to fall within the boundaries of religion, but not to teach a distillation or composite of them as a secular general religion. Scholars have never achieved consensus on the content of a "civil religion" nor does the religion of secular democracy of John Dewey commend itself as more than a useful generalization about the nobler side of the American mind. Where the schools teach the importance of participating in the democratic process, together with the values that support such participation, we do not discern religion, civil or otherwise. The teaching of basic social values—family life, civil obligations, economic justice—is not religion.

Profession of belief in God has widely different meanings to Americans. It appears to convey a sense that personal and social values are not grounded solely in the human mind but may stand in judgment of persons and society. In the prevalence of professed belief in God, however nominal, we discern society's struggle to stave off the divisiveness that engulfs a people among whom value consensus has failed. Whether this is "religion" or not may be a matter of definition. Certainly it is not Christ's unique call to repent and live in the kingdom of God.

We see no objection to the public authority's teaching a secular value consensus if there is one, but not as religion. A civil religion that is the product of abstraction from the historical faiths or an amalgam of common elements that eliminates the distinctive beliefs and moral teachings of each and that reinforces institutions favored by the dominant elites must be scrupulously opposed. It distorts the actual religions and debases religion itself by enlisting it in the service of state and society. To many Jews, Christians, and other believers the service of God above all other authorities is an evidence of true religion.

Public education is not the only institution in which the church encounters the problem of civil religion. Much preaching is inspired by an enthusiasm for the national way of life that owes more to secular idealism than to the Bible. Some argue that the role of the church leader in a pluralistic society includes not only the maintenance of congregational life within denominational boundaries but also support of the nation's social integrity by preaching public morals. The view taken here is that to abstract a public moral religion from the many currents of actual religion fails the test of truth-telling by assuming common beliefs that in fact are not shared by all. The most effective and honest way for the church to affect a whole society is to speak its convictions plainly, allowing personal religious faith to be either implicit or explicit as the subject may require, and never to pretend to speak for a religion of mere hypothesis.

Ministers should feel no hesitation to participate freely in public debate of issues both political, moral, and religious.

> *Following the death of his grandchild, this writer wrote an editorial for the local newspaper which argued that government intervention in decisions about life-support as proposed by the Department of Health and Human Services in 1983 intruded on the rights of the family and the obligations of the medical profession. The editorial said that "the medical profession, totally opposed to these wretched regulations, has proposed a set of ethical guidelines that express the best experience of years of decision making in one of life's most painful passages. . . . Those guidelines are right and . . . this latest example of governmental meddling in matters that by right belong within the family is utterly wrong."*

Here a clergyman offered a judgment on a matter fundamental to the well-being of any society: which of its components—government, family, or medical profession—has the right and duty to make such a decision?

There is a significant ethical difference between expressing a practical moral judgment of considerable consequence to the whole society and advocating a consensus-oriented modification of one's faith as a general answer to the moral dilemmas of society. The first does not involve any tampering with one's own beliefs or with the religious faith—or irreligiousness—of others, while the second forces religious beliefs, including ethical beliefs, through the screen of secular acceptability. To advocate some sort of civil religion when it represents the personal conviction of the advocate is certainly not dishonest but it may not be the proper task of the ordained.

## The Minister as a Public Servant

While some clergy become politicians or civil servants and discontinue the special functions to which they were ordained, practicing clergy may serve in public offices such as school board or city council, unpaid service on a public advisory commission, or short-term appointive positions.

There is an important distinction between service in positions that are tax-supported or, if unpaid, are part of the structure of government, and those that are not. Professors in state institutions, even while protected by traditional principles such as academic freedom, have obligations that differ from teachers in private academies. First among these is a general commitment to use power or influence in the interest of the whole public rather than favoring a preferred sector. The clergy may on occasion be on the state payroll as civil servants or professors in state universities, but ministers should never be among the hordes whose goal is to obtain public advantage for a few. Commitment to this principle of justice is an ethical imperative for clergy who would serve in government.

*During the 1920s the Ku Klux Klan had intimidated the Roman Catholics of the city of D. by hooded marches and a large encampment outside the city. The population was about evenly divided between Protestants and Catholics and the solution worked out was that the school board should have a Protestant majority, the city council a Catholic majority. The Catholic church maintained a large parochial school system where almost all Catholic children attended; the chairman of the city council was the mayor elected by the council.*

*Pastor C., a Lutheran, was well respected in the city. After his retirement he was elected to the city council and subsequently was asked if he would accept election as mayor. Fifty years had elapsed since the troubles of the 1920s; the proportion of Protestant and Catholic had remained about the same. The parochial schools had weakened by comparison with the public schools, which had refrained from introducing Protestant religious practices and had attracted many Catholic children.*

Prudential and ethical concerns unite in many decisions. Should the agreement of the 1920s be maintained? Some felt that trouble would follow its abandonment. Or had the social life of the town evolved to the point where the agreement was obsolete? How would the election of a Protestant minister to the mayor's office be understood?

Pastor C. was trusted by Catholic community leaders and the proposal that he should become mayor was not regarded as a sign of resurgent Protestant prejudice. He had long opposed the introduction of religious practices in the public schools on the ground that they would tend to polarize the public and parochial school systems. Finding that the community had left most of the old fears behind, he accepted election by the council, stating his intention to conduct the office in ways that would bring a half-century of division to a close.

Pastor C. saw here a ministry of reconciliation between social factions. He probably could not have accepted so large a public responsibility had he been a parish minister, if only because of limits on his time. Where public service takes substantial time, concern for equity requires the consent of the officers of the local church and/or the senior judicatory.

Public service, governmental or private and philanthropic, can be so compelling as to raise questions about the calling of the minister. Motivation and commitment to pastoral roles may wither. The ethical commitment to truth-telling—in this case, telling the whole truth to oneself—requires that the clergy be very clear about precisely what is going on, particularly if the pastoral vocation is giving way to another.

### Tent-making or Moonlighting?

Increasingly, circumstances are forcing clergy to augment income from business activity. Necessity may dictate it. When we disapprove such activity we call it "moonlighting"; when we accept it, it is "tent-making."

"Moonlighting" in the pejorative sense means taking time, perhaps surreptitiously, from pastoral work to earn money that may or may not be needed. "Tent-making" means self-support through secular work in order to finance a ministry that otherwise could not be undertaken or could be accomplished only at some risk of misunderstanding. The problems lie between these poles.

St. Paul argued that for the sake of his ministry he would take money from no one in compensation for his work—although he defended his right as an evangelist to the support of the church—but gained his living from his skill with the needle. This constitutes an ethical choice: is secular work designed to enable ministry and to protect its integrity or does it raise questions about the seriousness of a pastor's calling and commitment?

*John R. was pastor of a struggling city church in an area of declining population and great human need. The sponsoring judicatory could not increase its subsidy for this church's mission and the membership was no longer able to support the minimum salary requirement. Pastor R.'s needs were increasing: his wife had given birth to their third child. So Pastor R. accepted an opportunity to earn*

*supplementary income as a draftsman, a skill he had learned before
entering the ministry. He worked at home at times of his own
choosing.*

Several issues present themselves in this example. Pastor R. wanted to
establish the viability of the parish as a regularly supported judicatory
mission and did not want to change his job solely for financial reasons.
His secular work did not interfere with his schedule of pastoral work.
At the level of intention, the decision was ethically sound. However,
he did not discuss his secular employment opportunity with representatives of his congregation or the supporting judicatory. Assured of his
own calling, he saw no reason to believe that anyone would question
his decision.

If there was fault here, it lay primarily in Pastor R.'s assumption that
the central issue of the decision was the integrity of his calling. In fact
there were other issues involved, such as the responsibility of the congregation to its mission in the community, the duty of the judicatory
to consider further subsidy, and the responsibility of the officers of
church and judicatory to maintain full-time pastoral service. Pastor R.
would have been on sounder ground if he had taken an analysis of his
own needs to his congregation's officers and those of the judicatory and
sought their support in his decision to accept supplementary secular
work.

Such an approach is also necessary practically. A successor pastor
might not be able to work out the complex system of support on which
his congregation now depended for its pastor's services. Furthermore,
Pastor R. had solved a problem that, in addition to being personal, was
the church's and ought to have been addressed by the church.

Tent-making or moonlighting? Unwise tent-making may leave a parish weakened, however honest the intention of the pastor. Ethically
responsible thinking requires that clergy take account of all relevant
circumstances, including long-term effects.

Circumstances that call auxiliary employment into ethical question
include lack of candidness with one's principal employer about the time
demands of outside work and excessive withdrawal of time from the
pastoral task, and earning that is not strictly necessary to meet need.
In order to justify auxiliary employment, benefit must be demonstrated
for both congregation and the pastor's own career and family. It is a
proper concern of the church as well as the pastor that both needs be
met.

Pastoral work may be impossible in certain locales without a planned
tent-making ministry. Where full-time pastoral service is not required

and where none at all is possible without secular employment, or where the development of parish life and support depends on prompt part-time service, the tent-making approach is appropriate. The integrity of such undertakings is vindicated by the openness, thoughtfulness, and effectiveness of the decisions made.

## Relating to Other Professionals

The clergy share common ground with a broad range of professionals in the community. These other professionals may work alone but increasingly they work in teams, such as clinics, law partnerships, accounting firms, colleges. All too often they do not relate cordially or trustingly to other professions and professionals.

*Pastor T. was visiting an elderly member in the Veterans Administration hospital in his city. She was unsure of the precise health situation of her member and asked to see the physician. This doctor was an Asian, did not speak English fluently, and was scarcely civil to Pastor T. Who was she? What right had she to information about patients? Pastor T. identified herself and attempted to explain what pastors do. He also noted that the patient had a variety of needs that could best be met by the collaboration of professional persons. The response was cold. Pastor T. considered visiting the hospital administrator's office but decided she might better spend her time with her parishioners than hassling the Veterans Administration.*

While there are cultural obstacles to interprofessional communication, those who are puzzled about how to relate to other professionals often find that they behave in ways dictated more by personal predilections and temperament than by professional protocol. Yet pastors cannot perform their pastoral duties at maximum effectiveness if they have not worked out some way to communicate with doctors, attorneys, law enforcement personnel, and many others.

Beyond one-to-one relationships between professionals meeting in the course of their work, there is a larger sphere in which the professions themselves meet. Major social issues such as the life-centered questions (e.g., abortion, prolongation of life by heroic methods, the definition of death, genetic engineering), bring different groups of professionals together to meet with ethicists seeking to do what is right. Persons who attend conferences on such matters are obviously concerned and ready to communicate. Furthermore, sticky questions of confidentiality and other patient-related issues do not ordinarily arise; if they do, it is at the level of theory. Conversation with other professionals should be encouraged and attended by the clergy, both for information and also to understand the attitudes of other professionals.

Some of the principles held in common by professions should foster interprofessional communication. First among these is the conception of responsibility to the patient or client alone, safeguarded by the principle of confidentiality. Unfortunately doctors and lawyers only too often treat a call from a clergy person as a foray into someone else's business. Yet the prudent sharing of information among professionals is in the interest of the client. It is possible only in the presence of mutual trust. A minister should honor very strictly the shared professional standards: primary concern for the welfare of the counselee, patient, or client, confidentiality, and a high level of professional competence. All professions include practitioners who are weak in these fundamentals and their presence is a legitimate concern of ministers, doctors, or lawyers who are asked to consult with someone unknown to them. Still, with due caution, professionals should share such information as will enhance the care of the patient or client within the limits of confidentiality as defined by the profession itself.

There are interprofessional questions so inherently thorny that professionals are often thrown into conflict. A parishioner may seek counsel, for example, that puts a minister squarely between doctor and patient.

*A member of Pastor B.'s congregation was being treated for a condition known to be serious. The doctor was somewhat authoritarian and expected his patient to accept his judgments without explanation of the treatment. The patient very much wanted to know what was going on and confided her frustration to her pastor. Pastor B. needed guidance about the whole question of intervening in the relationship between the parishioner and her doctor.*

The interest of the patient is controlling. To be sure, a doctor may have medical (rather than temperamental) reasons for saying little about treatment; yet the patient's rights are primary. She alone has the final right to decide what interventions in her body, medical or surgical, are appropriate and she is therefore entitled to understand her illness. It is unprofessional and unethical to deny her the knowledge needed to exercise that right. The pastor would be correct in supporting her demand for information and her right to decide. Failing her doctor's response, he should encourage her to change to another physician. The resultant conflict, if any, would be an acceptable consequence of ethically correct behavior.

Conflicts between professional interests and between professionals themselves are complex.

*Dr. X., a member of Pastor S.'s church, had been treating a patient, also a member, for nervous tension. After considerable time, the symptoms proved to be caused by a heart condition. A few months later, the patient died of a heart attack. His family filed a malpractice suit. Pastor S. is concerned for her members' suffering grief and conflict; she is also aware that large damage awards have become a problem in themselves. Notwithstanding the mistaken diagnosis, she believes the doctor is competent, but not infallible. How shall she deal with the conflict between her members while bringing them pastoral care?*

Pastor S. would be well-advised to seek help from an attorney concerned with medical malpractice. What is the history of these suits? Are physician's defenses usually successful? Are they often settled out of court? What would be considered a fair settlement? Her members may never invite her to discuss the lawsuit but she must be well informed if any opportunity to play a reconciling role should present itself. She needs also to know how the medical profession and individual doctors react to malpractice suits. If the doctor should wish to discuss the question, the minister could easily find herself in over her head. In dealing with the grieving family she may find that the suit is partly an expression of the generalized anger normal in grief. To help the family cope with grief would be a reconciling response, whether or not the lawsuit were ever discussed.

Experienced pastors will understand that they need to know a great deal when such discussions come up: the inherent difficulty of diagnosing certain conditions accurately and the frequency of error in estimating the life expectancy of patients with heart conditions such as the deceased's (both with and without treatment), circumstances in the family that may compound the emotional difficulties of grief, and much more. A pastor needs to be apt in discovering ways that discussion of the conflict can be turned toward reconciliation and to be patient in awaiting the precisely right time to turn discussion in that direction. As hard as it is to know all that one must know in order to perform effectively in interprofessional matters, pastors have an ethical responsibility to master the relevant information. There is no way to "wing it."

Professionals can be brought together by patients whose needs demand interdisciplinary competences.

*Pastor L. had been counseling a parishioner with a history of emotional disturbance. She was worried because the parishioner had been expressing suicidal wishes. The pastor believed that psychiatric evaluation and perhaps treatment were needed but she could not persuade her counselee, who distrusted psychiatrists and all their works.*

Distrust is often a problem of those who seek help and pastors and they must be very careful to preserve the fragile base of trust offered them. This calls for great care in sharing confidential information with fellow professionals, even in the interest of the patient. Yet Pastor L. had also to consider her moral and legal responsibility in case the counselee should carry out the threat of suicide. This would suggest that importance of consulting a psychiatrist for advice without identifying the counselee.

# 10

# The Professional Character

The professional ethic of the clergy—indeed, the distinctive person-hood of the minister—is found in the mystery of vocation: the con-viction of the church that God speaks authoritatively through God's own people to the individual persons who compose it. For Christians, ethics, including professional ethics, is drawn from the Word of God.

No learning, no discipline, no skilled professionalism of itself gives life to the practice of the ministry. Indeed, there is something wryly anomalous about ordained sinners seeking to become accomplished prophets, teachers, and priests. The figure of the Pharisee warns us: the person who knows how to pray expertly is the Pharisee. Only if there is something of the hopelessly unprofessional publican within can one hope for authenticity in the clergy life.

Any human being immersed every day in the practice of a profession continuously experiences the impact of professional demands upon the self. The mature professional is a person who has grown through this process without sacrificing individuality and personal integrity.

An authentic professional ethic is simply the system of behavior freely adopted by a called person. That behavior in turn expresses a view of life rooted in deeply felt convictions. A mature ethic possesses power to integrate its bearers with their social and cultural environ-ments. Such an ethic is not produced by the experience of a moment or deduced from a single commanding belief. Much less is it the creation of a committee. It expresses a human being's total moral development. Responsible professional behavior is the product of a prolonged and continuing process of personal formation.

## The Professional Personality

A mature professional has internalized both the demands and limits of professional life to the point of behaving ethically most of the time as though by instinct. The formation of professional personhood is a highly creative process. "Professional development" sometimes denotes the amassing of continuing education credits. Here we mean the lifelong evolution of commitments in the form of disciplined habits and their corollary skills. The semblance of a professional may be produced by imposing specific behaviors and cultivating special attitudes but authentic professional character is independent and creative, not passive and plastic. Eliza Doolittle's education at the hand of Professor 'iggins is not the sort of process that makes responsible professionals.

The ministry is not defined by its subject matter but by its vocation. A person considering entering the ministry is beginning to grasp the church's belief that the body of God's people and all its professional servants exist only because God summons them to service. Candidates for church vocations gradually learn to participate in the church's reflection on its origin and faith. Within that context, they begin to develop professional personhood. Naive first articulations of the call develop until ministers and professionals in ministry come to a more complex understanding of their special functions within the called community.

A church profession is spiritual before it is knowledgeable or skillful. The maturing church professional is above all a person who lives from the conviction that God is the actuator of life in the faith community and of the selfhood of the clergy.

The word "spiritual" is anathema to some in the Christian community because of its association with pious pretension and inauthenticity. But it is used here to denote the distinguishing criterion of the church professions: the conviction that neither church nor any church office would or could exist unless God had created it. Ordination, like the church, rests on an act of God. The special education and ethical standards of church leaders flow from that. All ministry is an act of divine grace before it is a human endeavor. Anything a pastor or other church professional does is a response to God before it is a human initiative. The entry of God's Spirit into the human spirit actuates the gifts of human creativity in the highest degree. Grace calls forth the latent powers of the human person; the initiative of God blesses the talents of believers.

The spiritual heart of the ministry of the church is the awareness that a divine activity infuses and surrounds it. Church professionals know that God deals with their weaknesses—the Pharisee in them, the ebb and flow of spiritual self-awareness, their vanity and vulnerability, their experiences of dryness. They know the history of God's people and how God never ceased to return to them. The spiritual life of all the called is antecedent to every other truth about the profession. Liveliness in this faith is its primary qualification and its distinguishing characteristic among the professions.

The clergy and its lay associates in ministry are not a product of institutional influences, however significant. But it takes nothing from the authenticity of calling to recognize its dependence on means: family values, an admired minister, the persuasions of an adult who discerns in a young person special possibilities, and education.

Seminaries are often held responsible for the quality of the clergy and this is not altogether mistaken. But before a seminary ever receives a candidate, spiritual formation is well advanced. Professional character is profoundly influenced by the integrity of the candidate's models. Such impressions are indispensable, unavoidable, and ineradicable. The young minister who loves center stage has not been made so by a seminary, although seminary leaders may have lacked the insight or courage to challenge traits that handicap an otherwise promising talent. The vanities that cripple ministers and afflict congregations are often products of fundamental bents of personality. The best human materials that seminaries work with may be substantially the result of the spiritual life of family and congregation.

## The Professional at Work: An Example

So complete is the union of training, ethic, and personhood in the mature professional that these may not be readily distinguishable to the observer. We here cite a very personal experience of one of the authors to clarify the way in which a thoroughly internalized professional ethic actually works.

*In October of 1982 my daughter gave birth to her first child, a nine-pound boy. During labor the placenta detached. As promptly as the surgeon reacted, the Caesarian section was too late and the child was born in a coma.*

*After the baby had been in intensive care for forty-eight hours, time enough for evaluation, my son-in-law and I conferred with a group consisting of a neurologist (the senior member of the team),* three neo-natologists, and the nurse attending the baby. First, there was a full report on the condition of the baby. In substance, the trend of his vital functions was steadily downward. Experience indicated that the two or three percent who come out of post-natal coma trend upward during the first two days.

Second, the implications of these facts meant that it was impossible to say whether he would remain in coma or even if he would live. Neurological tests showed no hearing, sight, or voluntary movement of the body. Yet it was impossible to predict with certainty that he would die. The doctors recounted instances of children in virtually identical situations who had lived fifteen years or longer. We had the "Karen Quinlan problem."

There was also the intimidating shadow of the law. My son-in-law and I had entered the conference wondering if the doctors were practicing "defensive medicine." We learned that the laws of Pennsylvania did not apply clearly to the choices we had to make. I assured the doctors that we found no fault in the medical procedures, and that the emotional circumstances in the family created no inclination toward a malpractice suit. Their response was to explain the policy processes to which they were bound when the issue was life itself. A conference such as we were involved in was required first. Then, if necessary, consultation with a hospital committee and clearance with the hospital's legal counsel would be the next step. As a last resort, the family could petition for a court order permitting removal of life support. The child was actually not in our custody, nor even the doctor's. He was already protected by the state. All this we dreaded. The leader of the medical group then stated: "Our stance is that whatever we all agree on may be done within the bounds of our professional responsibility. If we agree, none of these complications need arise."

Suffusing this entire conversation was a manifest compassion for us that made their very competence comforting. In their own way, they too were suffering: They lacked power to save the child. I offered what comfort I could by telling them that for us, given our understanding of life, death was not ultimate. The youngest of the doctors replied: "For you that is true, Dr. Smith; but for us, death is defeat."

My daughter had already agreed that in these circumstances life support should be ended. "If the baby cannot live on his own, he should not live." The doctors told the nurses that any who wished to

*be transferred until the baby died might be reassigned (none asked),*
*and life support was removed.*
   *The next day the baby died.*

While this story exhibits an application of medical guidelines, more significantly it lays open the meaning of professional character. The behavior of these medical professionals may be described as a series of movements between polarities that complement one another—competence and compassion.

Competence stands in the forefront, complemented by compassion. The world of technique offers a certain shelter to people who wish to avoid the pain of shared emotion. For this reason "competence" sometimes implies coldness. But only people are cold. Since knowledge often grants a vision of suffering to come, it might be supposed that to know the effects of fatal illness would excite compassion. This is true of the mature professional whose technical competence is coupled with compassion at every step of practice. The professional does not work alone, however much time may be spent in study and laboratory, but with human beings in their wholeness.

Ministers, like physicians, must find ways to protect themselves from the powerful emotion often associated with their ministries. There are some occupations in which there is low emotional involvement either with the work or the people who are being served. Administrative skills, demanded by a developing congregation, for example, involve knowledge that is not in itself emotionally charged. Yet rounded pastoral ministry cannot be competently performed without the emotional maturity required to accept the pain of the persons to whom one ministers. At the same time, the danger that emotional involvement may injure professional effectiveness is at least as great for the clergy as for other professionals.

## Compassion and Distance

Professionals who are only ambiguously committed to the good of their clients, patients, or church members may rightly be criticized. Compassion is an important force producing this commitment. At the same time, the professional cannot function effectively unless a certain distance is maintained. Distance between counselor and counselee is the necessary partner of professional commitment. The mastery of behavior that takes form around the polarity of compassion and distance is a mark of professional character.

Counselees are often quite unclear about the distance that must be maintained and the professional must assume responsibility.

*Mrs. B. attended regularly a class conducted by the pastor of her church. She said little but finally confided to him that she had never loved her husband and asked what she should do.*

*Her parents, she said, were emotionally unstable and their conflict had been very scarring for her. She had been unable to commit herself emotionally to her husband at first but assumed love would come in time. It had not. His sexual behavior seemed self-centered to her and she said she did not feel loved. After several counseling sessions with her pastor she suddenly remarked: "I've never committed adultery but I know one older man with whom I would go to bed if he'd ask me." The pastor replied: "That would be a very complicated thing to do, wouldn't it?" and suggested that people in her situation usually benefit from simplifying their lives.*

*By the time the interview ended, the pastor had awakened to the possibility that he was himself the "older man" of whom she spoke. He wondered whether he had failed in some way to maintain the distance necessary to a sound counseling relation.*

The breakdown of general standards of propriety, not to say fundamental morality, throughout modern society has made this kind of counselee behavior very prevalent. The same social forces invite undisciplined response.

The ability to maintain an appropriate distance, although no more essential for female professionals than for males, is underlined by the increase of unmarried ordained women in the ministry. Many complain of sexual exploitation by male clergy. In present circumstances the female clergy must define professional distance in specific relation to the sexual factor. In a generation in which so many are encountering female clergy for the first time, it is particularly important to convince men that ordained women are to be regarded and treated as persons and professionals, and also to establish trust among the women of the congregation.

Without distance, compassion is corrupted. A mature professional does not see compassion as constrained by distance. Psychological distance actually gives room for the labors of compassion and protects both the counselee and the pastor from forces that threaten to falsify professional service. A mature professional possesses the ability to project concern that unites compassion with appropriate distance.

## Self-interest and Service

No one invests years in educational preparation without being concerned to measure up to general expectations of good performance. This inevitably thrusts self-interest into the practice of any profession. Yet the very touchstone of being a professional is service. Service is the foundation of public respect for professional people. The public is very sensitive to the tension between service and self-interest and greed is widely charged against affluent professionals.

A religious professional is probably more deeply damaged than any other by the suspicion of undue concern for financial gain. In this matter the tension between self-interest and service easily grows into pure contradiction. The clergy cannot demand to be ministered unto, however important fair compensation for services may be.

The reconciliation of an appropriate self-interest with the commitment to service depends on the manner in which self-concern shapes conduct and how that conduct is understood.

A prime example is the way the clergy respond to the tax laws. The tax laws pose not only the personal ethical question of honesty in reporting income and expense but also sharply raise the issue of justice. The ethical issues posed by taxation are not resolved by submitting a defensible tax return. Legislators have introduced a system of exemptions—called "loopholes" by those who dislike them—deliberately designed to allocate economic advantage and some of these benefit the clergy.

Every minister who owns a home is aware that there is a double deduction for interest on home mortgages. The first is the exemption of housing allowances from income tax; the second, the legality of deducting interest on mortgages from taxable income. It is the same money twice subtracted for the purpose of computing tax liability. This practice was ended before the new legislation of 1986, but has now been reinstated.

The deductible housing allowance is a carryover from the era when a house was almost always provided for the minister's use. The tax law translated this into a deduction of substitute income. But to permit in addition the deduction of an amount equivalent to interest paid on a mortgage is clearly a special benefit.

The ethically concerned minister had three choices: (1) to take both deductions on the assumption that the Congress intended a special benefit for clergy; (2) to refuse the interest deduction and pay the tax on that amount; or (3) to take the deduction as provided by law but to urge that the loophole be closed. (Opponents of all taxation or those protesting the application of tax money to military or other uses would make other choices.)

The issue that concerns us here is whether the clergy will choose solely according to self-interest or will take into account the impact of its decision on the practice of ministry. There is more involved here than money! Confidence in the integrity of the clergy is essential to its effectiveness.

Tax decisions are but one example of the broad range of professional activity dealing with self-interest and service. Is the Christian education director who is absent from the congregation two to four weeks a year (in addition to vacation time) in order to foster professional development acting in the interest of the church? How about the minister in poor health who is hanging on until sixty-five while rendering less service than the congregation needs? Debate concerning such behaviors may move between the poles of self-interest and service, and some problems cannot be resolved without taking account of other norms as well. For example, pastors or those involved in professional ministry who allocate time to studies that would otherwise be spent in parish service may be working toward long-range vocational objectives that will enhance their usefulness through a specialized ministry. In effect, one congregation's disadvantage may work to the benefit of another. The question here is fairness and proportion. The minister in declining health may believe that other relevant considerations, such as the completion of a program crucial for the congregation's future, create a balance favorable to his continuing even when handicapped. Professional character asserts itself definitively in difficult times of choice.

## Public Role and the Integrity of the Person

We have already discussed the importance of setting aside a certain amount of time during which the mind can do its work unpressed by deadlines and worries. It is obligatory to foster conditions that favor one's saying within oneself: "Very well now, the real truth is . . ." followed by the act of telling oneself the truth and putting an end to the rationalizations and self-justifications that falsify ethical thinking. We are dealing with the elemental question of the integrity of the person. There are irrepressible forces within most people that push them in directions they do not yet understand. From such inner ferment come decisions to make fundamental life changes in vocation, life-style, and marital directions. Many an apparently successful professional career or marriage has been jettisoned or destroyed by the sudden explosion of long-repressed psychic forces. Professional practice itself generates pressures that must be dealt with personally and within the family. In this perspective, it is ethically essential to reserve private time to deal with oneself, and one's spouse and children for the sake of both the self and the integrity of professional practice.

For the clergy and church professional, resolution of the polarity between public life and the need for integrity in private life is complicated by the difficulty of keeping them apart. People know what their minister is doing! A pastor or church professional may feel pressed to justify time "taken from" ministry, as it is often regarded. And so privacy is sacrificed. As for the minister's family, people know a great deal about it, too: its recreational interests, possessions, problems. A minister is only too easily put on the defensive about an unusual recreational interest, or what a son or daughter is doing.

Professionals themselves are sometimes responsible for this intrusion of public life upon privacy. One example of this is the well-known custom of taking the day's load of tension home and dumping it on the family. To be sure, a major contribution of a spouse to the professional effectiveness of the partner may be to listen and respond in ways that help to moderate emotion and to develop sound judgments. With the consent of the spouse this is partnership in profession, not mere dumping. There is a role for the husband or wife of the professional in the nourishment of a healthy distinction between public and private life, lest the human being simply disappear into the maw of the public figure. In principle, church people are quick to affirm the importance of "taking time for the family"—but they may nevertheless be offended to find their ministers unavailable when they need them. Ministers need to take the initiative in explaining what private time is all about so that they may avoid the trap of self-justification and defensiveness.

Many of the gifts necessary in professional practice are subject to abuse. Discretion is essential to protect privacy—but at an extreme it can become secretiveness. Candidness affirms openness but unaccompanied by discretion can become offensive. Honesty is essential but when evoked to justify rudeness, insensitivity, or mere assertiveness, honesty is less than a virtue. Humor enables people to endure the ambiguity of life and affirms openness between people but it may also be cruel or even vulgar. A mature person is aware of these issues. The professional person recognizes them as ethical choices that may enable or handicap effectiveness in service.

"The new man [sic] in Christ finds not a rigid set of maxims to be applied casuistically but a living Lord to be followed dynamically."[1] This maxim reminds us that the professional character is profoundly formed "in Christ," not forced into the straitjacket of an approved code of ethics. In this world, the comfort of knowing oneself to be right is denied to all but the Pharisees among us. No individual can evade responsibility for ethical decision. The person and words of Christ declare the perfections of life in his kingdom. They point directions, set limits, and profoundly shape the mind of the professional clergy along with all dwellers in God's earthly kingdom. To live confidently and faithfully with incompleteness, risk, and ambiguity in the name of one's Lord is to become the kind of person demanded by the religious professions.

# Notes

## Introduction

1. Much was written on ministerial ethics in the 1920s and 1930s. The literature then died away for reasons unknown. In the last decade the subject has again begun to receive attention. Two books have treated it in the context of professional ethics in general: Darrell Reeck, *Ethics for the Professions: A Christian Perspective* (Minneapolis: Augsburg, 1982); and Dennis M. Campbell, *Doctors, Lawyers, Ministers: Christian Ethics in Professional Practice* (Nashville: Abingdon Press, 1982). Karen Lebacqz's fine book, *Professional Ethics: Power and Paradox* (Nashville: Abingdon Press, 1985), focuses especially upon ethics for clergy but does not attempt to cover the range of particular situations and problems that we have included in this book.

2. David Luban, ed., *The Good Lawyer: Lawyers' Roles and Lawyers' Ethics* (Totowa, N.J.: Rowan and Allenheld, 1984), 1.

3. For help in such problems, see Lindell L. Gumper, *Legal Issues in the Practice of Ministry* (Detroit: Harlo Printing Co., 1981); William H. Tiemann, *The Right to Silence: Privileged Clergy Communication and the Law* (Nashville: Abingdon Press, 1983); Richard R. Hammar, *Pastor, Church and Law* (Springfield, Mo.: Gospel Publishing House, 1983); H. Newton Malony, Thomas L. Needham, and Samuel Southard, *Clergy Malpractice* (Philadelphia: Westminster Press, 1986).

4. See the discussion of truth-telling in chap. 1.

## Chapter 1: What Is Telling the Truth?

1. This essay is reproduced in James M. Gustafson and James T. Laney, eds., *On Being Responsible* (New York: Harper & Row, 1968), 120–26, together with the contrasting essay by Dietrich Bonhoeffer, "What Is Meant by 'Telling the Truth'?" to which we shall refer below. The editors' introduction to the essays (pp. 111–19) should be read. Kant's essay is taken from Lewis White

Beck, ed., *The Critique of Practical Reason and Other Writings on Moral Philosophy* (Chicago: University of Chicago Press, 1949), 346–50.

2. "He grew up in a Moravian household. He was a Christian and he thought as a Christian, though not in theological terms" (Paul Lehmann, *Ethics in a Christian Context* [London: SCM, 1963], 128).

3. It has been noted that this statement occurs nowhere in Kant's writings. Kant is quoting a contemporary philosopher, Benjamin Constant, who does not actually name Kant as the source. Kant seems to have acknowledged that it does represent his view, however, and proceeds to defend it.

4. In fact, Kant offers another sort of justification for his view of truthtelling, one that does not seem to be consistent with his basic approach to ethics. He actually does take account of the consequences or effects of lying, though of general and long-range effects. Lying, he argues, always does harm. He maintains that a society requires laws and that a legal system must be based upon a principle of absolute truthfulness. Persons must be accountable for what they say, for instance in commitments made when they enter into contracts. Allowing exceptions—in effect, excusing lies—will undermine the very basis of law. Thus lying always does harm to humanity generally, even if it does not harm an individual in a particular case. But an appeal to harm done is an appeal to consequences. This is inconsistent with the idea that principles (in Kant's language, *a priori* and apodictic principles) must be obeyed from a sense of duty only, without regard to consequences.

5. Dietrich Bonhoeffer, *Ethics*, ed. Eberhard Bethge (New York: Macmillan & Co., 1965), 363–72.

6. For an account of this notion of "Christ reality" in Bonhoeffer, see Larry Rasmussen, *Dietrich Bonhoeffer: Reality and Resistance* (Nashville: Abingdon Press, 1972).

7. See the letter of December 1943, appended to the essay in Bonhoeffer, *Ethics*, 371f.

8. Lehmann, *Ethics in a Christian Context*, 129. The relevant passage from Lehmann is reproduced in Gustafson and Laney, *On Being Responsible*, 136–45.

9. Ibid., p. 130. Quite possibly, what Lehmann intends is that parties to a good relationship would acknowledge this and sense intuitively what sort of veracity was needed, so that the issue would really take care of itself.

10. Cf. Kant's essay in Gustafson and Laney, *On Being Responsible*, 125.

11. "Human intellectual ingenuity can best be measured by our apparently unlimited ability to invent justifications for what we have done or want to do"— Wiest's Law.

12. To show further Bonhoeffer's serious concern about veracity, we note that he allows the child in school to tell a factual lie but indicates that one must make allowance for the child's immaturity. An adult in a parallel situation would be able to avoid an outright lie by pointing out that the questioner was out of line and giving the reasons for believing so.

13. While this item in Bonhoeffer's thought requires an understanding of his ethics overall and its interrelations with his personal experiences, the essence of it might be found in the sections of his *Ethics* under the headings "Acceptance of Guilt," "Conscience," and "Freedom."

14. H. Richard Niebuhr, who did not scorn the help that principles or rules can give, was right nevertheless in maintaining that following rules must be put in the context of the overarching responsiveness of persons to persons when decisions are made. See H. Richard Niebuhr, *The Responsible Self* (New York: Harper & Row, 1978). On the whole debate over the relation of principles to contexts, see James Gustafson's fine and still useful article, "Context vs. Principles: A Misplaced Debate in Christian Ethics" (*Harvard Theological Review* 58/2 [April 1965]), republished in James M. Gustafson, *Christian Ethics and the Community* (Philadelphia: United Church Press, 1979), 101–26.

15. Article on "Truth" by Otto A. Piper in *The Interpreter's Dictionary of the Bible*, vol. 4, George A. Buttrick, ed. (Nashville: Abingdon Press, 1962), 713–17.

16. Walter Bauer, *A Greek-English Lexicon of the New Testament and Other Early Christian Literature*, trans. and adapt. William F. Arndt and F. Wilbur Gingrich (Chicago: University of Chicago Press, 1952), 35.

17. E. C. Blackman, "Truth," in *A Theological Word Book of the Bible*, ed. Alan Richardson (New York: Macmillan, 1959), 270.

18. And with Spirit also (cf. 1 John 5:7).

19. Blackman, "Truth," 270.

20. Piper, "Truth," 4:715, 717.

## Chapter 2: How We Tell the Truth

1. *The American Heritage Dictionary*, Second College Edition (Boston: Houghton Mifflin, 1982, 1985), 946.

2. H. Richard Niebuhr, *Radical Monotheism and Western Culture* (New York: Harper & Bros., 1960), chap. 2.

3. While one would not overload a sermon with references to scholarly writers whose names mean nothing to laity, still one can be too shy about such things. References designed to familiarize laity with the names and ideas of certain theological scholars past and present are not bad if kept within reason. Such references are all the more productive when coupled with an effective program of education in the local church.

4. We are indebted for this reference to Dr. Arthur W. Lindsley, Jr., who has included it in his unpublished doctoral dissertation, *Conscience and Casuistry in the English Puritan Concept of Reformation* (Pittsburgh: University of Pittsburgh, 1982), 224–26.

5. For an interesting discussion of this point, see Lon Fuller, *The Morality of Law*, rev. ed. (New Haven: Yale University Press, 1969), chap. 1.

6. There is a legitimate concept of "continuing revelation," but to define and defend it would not be pertinent here.

7. Martin Buber, A *Prophetic Faith* (New York: Macmillan and Co., 1949).

8. The case is *Tarasoff vs. Regents of the University of California* (17 California Reports, 3rd Series, 425). For one discussion of it, see Tom L. Beauchamp and James F. Childress, *Principles of Biomedical Ethics*, second edition (New York: Oxford University Press, 1983), 281–84.

## Chapter 3: The Authority of the Minister

1. See Edward Schillebeeckx, *Ministry* (New York: Crossroad Publishing Co., 1981), and also the modified and extended version of the thesis in Edward Schillebeeckx, *The Church with a Human Face* (New York: Crossroad, 1985).

2. The Scriptural basis for this, of course, is Rom. 12:3-8 and 1 Cor. 12:4-13 in which there is reference to "varieties of ministry."

3. Schillebeeckx, *Ministry*, 68.

4. Christian faith and life are "in Christ" and being "in Christ" means also being incorporated into his body, the church, of which he is head. Our ministry is participation in Christ's own ministry or service. Thus in the most fundamental sense it may be said, as T. F. Torrance has in fact done, that it is Christ who ordains. T. F. Torrance, *Conflict and Agreement in the Church*, Vol. 2 (London: Lutterworth Press, 1960), 46.

5. Schillebeeckx, *Ministry*, 66f. The author sees evidences of a reaffirmation of the first, earlier view in Vatican II documents but says that the relevant statements in the documents actually mix elements of both views so that the earlier one has not been fully recovered.

6. Ibid., 69f.

7. Ibid., 73.

8. Mark 10:42-45; Matt. 20:25-28.

9. This is discussed further in chap. 9, 170.

10. Karl Barth, *Church Dogmatics*, vol. IV (Edinburgh: T. & T. Clark, 1956); cited in Robert Clyde Johnson, ed., *The Church and Its Changing Ministry* (Philadelphia: Office of the General Assembly, United Presbyterian Church, U.S.A., 1961). See also the useful selections in Ray S. Anderson, ed., *The Theological Foundations for Ministry* (Grand Rapids, Mich.: Wm. B. Eerdmans, 1979), especially #17, "The Community for the World."

11. Such a dispute is also the occasion for similar statements in Luke 9:46-48 and Mark 9:33-37, where Jesus uses a little child to illustrate unpretentiousness and humility.

12. John 13:1-20.

13. John 13:13-15.

14. For a fine discussion of Jesus as example see James Gustafson, *Christ and the Moral Life* (New York: Harper & Row, 1968; reprint, University of Chicago Press, 1979).

15. Torrance, *Conflict and Agreement*, 44.

16. See Calvin, *Institutes of the Christian Religion* (Philadelphia: Westminster Press, 1960), IV.iii.4; iv.1.

17. See the excerpt from Karl Barth, *Church Dogmatics* IV/2 (Edinburgh: T. & T. Clark, 1956), 690–95; reproduced in Ray S. Anderson, ed., *Theological Foundations for Ministry*, 707–13.

18. Barth, *Church Dogmatics*, vol. I (Edinburgh: T. & T. Clark, English translation 1975), 88–124. Barth found precedent for these distinctions in various theological sources but especially in Luther. See 121–23. (For reference to the 1936 English translation, see 98–140 and 137–39.)

19. Matt. 25:31-46.

20. Joseph Sittler, "The Maceration of the Minister," in *The Christian Century* (10 June 1959), 698–701; reprinted in Robert C. Johnson, ed., *The Church and Its Changing Ministry*, 79–81.

21. F. Raymond Marks and Darlene Cathcart, "Discipline within the Legal Profession: Is It Self-Regulation?" Research Contributions of the American Bar Foundation, 1974, no. 5; reprinted from *Illinois Law Forum*, 1974, no. 2.

22. Luke 12:49; Matt. 10:34.

23. See the article, "When the Shepherd Strays. . . ," *The National Observer* (27 Dec. 1975), 12.

## Chapter 4: The Pastor as Professional

1. We cannot attempt any really thorough treatment of this subject here. This summary relies on brief accounts in Darrell Reeck, *Ethics for the Professions: A Christian Perspective* (Minneapolis: Augsburg, 1982), and James D. Glasse, *Profession: Ministry* (Nashville: Abingdon Press, 1968). For the essential elements in a definition of "profession" and "professional" see also Karen Lebacqz, *Professional Ethics: Power and Paradox* (Nashville: Abingdon Press, 1985), chap. 4. References in these books will provide a beginning bibliography for those who wish to pursue the subject further, as to both history and theoretical problems.

2. "Helps to define" is a phrase chosen to allow for the fact that the state has authority in such matters through licensure and otherwise. It has been pointed out recently, e.g., that legal ethics are really under the authority of the courts and not ultimately that of the American Bar Association. See T. Lumbard, "Setting Standards," *Catholic University Law Review* 2 (Winter 1981). The Association nevertheless formulates a code of professional ethics and state bar associations administer examinations for admission to the bar.

3. Glasse, *Profession: Minister*, 26–28.

4. Hans Küng, *The Church* (Garden City, N.Y.: Image Books, Doubleday & Co., 1976).

5. Ibid., 494.

6. Ibid., 502.

7. Ibid., 503.

8. Ibid., 486–88.

9. Glasse, *Profession: Minister*, chap. 6.

10. Küng, *The Church*, 483.

11. Ibid., 564f.

12. Hendrick Kraemer, *Theology of the Laity* (Philadelphia: Westminster Press, 1958).

13. There is a perennial problem about how to define such gifts in distinction from and/or in relation to "natural talents." Most theologies agree that they are not simply identical. On the other hand, a person who claims a gift for a ministry of music, for example, who has no "ear" for it should be guided gently but firmly into another kind of ministry. Talents and gifts relate to the "call" to the ministry, of which we shall say more below.

## Chapter 5: Practicing the Pastor's Authority

1. On this see Richard Hofstadter, *Anti-Intellectualism in America* (New York: Alfred A. Knopf, 1962).

2. We cannot overlook the overtones of sexuality here. Where there is a man as pastor, some women in the congregation will have a sort of "crush" on him. Since our sexuality is part of our being, this sort of reaction is not necessarily fatal to effective pastoral service but the pastor needs to be aware of what is going on. What may happen as congregations become more accustomed to women in clerical ministry is not yet fully known. We assume and hope that most pastors have some awareness of these overtones and some competence to deal with them. Such is our ineluctable humanity, however, that instances of pastors forsaking their marriages for relationships with others in the congregations are unfortunately only too familiar. Even if the situation does not come to this, pastors need always to be aware of the increment of sexuality, especially in some responses of a particularly flattering sort.

3. In this section we are indebted to insights published in *The National Observer* (27 Dec. 1975) article to which we have previously referred. Some of the suggestions about clergy ethics that the article contains were made by theologians but it is significant that many were made by Protestant pastors, Catholic priests, and rabbis. The insights are subtle and searching but often not readily verifiable. They are intended as questions to which clerics are invited to respond by posing them to see where the shoe fits.

## Chapter 6: The Pastor as Human Being

1. David Luban, ed., *The Good Lawyer: Lawyers' Roles and Lawyers' Ethics* (Totowa, N.J.: Rowan and Allanheld, 1984), 1–2.

2. Ibid., 2.

3. Ibid., 294f.

4. Karen Lebacqz, *Professional Ethics: Power and Paradox* (Nashville: Abingdon Press, 1985).

5. Ibid., 38.

6. We make use of Tillich's polarity between individualization and participation. For human beings, this becomes a tension between person and community. We refine it further, envisioning a tension between particular persons (clergy) and the roles assigned them by particular religious communities (their congregations and denominations).

7. Robert S. Paul, in his book *The Church in Search of Itself* (Grand Rapids, Mich.: Wm. B. Eerdmans, 1972) proposes that churches today should adopt a "tent-making" form of ministry combining partial church support with part-time secular occupations (see chap. 9, especially 347–51.) We agree with much of his view of what church and ministry are meant to be but think he leans too far toward applying St. Paul's model of church and ministry to different social circumstances. As he says himself, we should be open to the Spirit's moving to "initiate new forms of ministry (and) adapt new forms to changing conditions" (330). We see "tent-making" as appropriate in some situations but not a feasible basic pattern for our churches today.

## Chapter 8: The Ethics of a Worldly Church

1. We agree with the verdict of the majority of NewTestament scholars that the thesis of S. G. F. Brandon and others, that Jesus advocated political revolution of a sort comparable to the program of the Zealots, cannot be upheld. This does not mean, however, that revolution can never be a valid Christian option. We think such a choice can sometimes be right. Those American Protestants who might demur should ask themselves how they feel about the American Revolution—though it presents less ground for justification than do some situations in, for example, Latin America today.

## Chapter 9: Ministers and Social Establishments

1. A *Draught of the Form of the Government and Discipline of the Presbyterian Church in the United States of America* (New York and London, 1787), p. iii. Cf. *The Constitution of the United Presbyterian Church in the United States of America; The Book of Confessions* (Philadelphia, 1966).

## Chapter 10: The Professional Character

1. *Relations Between Church and State.* Text drafted by Benjamin Reist. Minutes of the General Assembly of the United Presbyterian Church. 1963.

# Index

CPSIA information can be obtained at www.ICGtesting.com
Printed in the USA
LVOW12s1552290414

383727LV00016B/1

3 4711 00219 4985

9 780800 623913